GIVEN to LOVE

St. Ambrose on the Pursuit of Chastity

Scepter

 Sermons preached by St. Ambrose at Milan and written out in three books (*de virginibus*) for his sister Marcellina, on the feast of Saint Agnes, 377 A.D. With a fourth book of other sermon notes (*de Virginitate*).

Translated by James Shiel.

Scripture quotations are the author's translation of the original text of St. Ambrose and thus do not match any known Scripture text. Quotations from the Psalms correspond to the numbering system for the RSVCE translation.

Nihil Obstat: Dionysius Vaughan, *censor theol. Deput.*

Imprimatur: John Carroll, archbishop of Dublin and Primate of Ireland, Dublin, March 27, 1963

Published by Scepter Publishers, Inc
info@scepterpublishers.org
www.scepterpublishers.org
800-322-8773
New York

Cover image from Wikimedia Commons
Cover design by Rose Design
Page design and pagination by Rose Design

ISBN (pbk): 9781594174780
ISBN (ebook): 9781594174797

Printed in the United States of America

CONTENTS

FOREWORD TO THE PRESENT EDITION (2023)

CHRISTIANITY CAME INTO ITS SECOND GENERATION of peaceful life following three hundred years of persecution, when Saint Ambrose (339–397) first preached in Milan to women and men about the single state of service to the Lord. Ambrose was 38 years old, the former prefect of Roman authority in the province surrounding Milan. Although born on the Roman frontier in Trier, Germany, he was brought to Rome for his education by his widowed mother.

In Rome he studied law, literature, and most importantly, rhetoric, and like his father in Trier, became the prefect of the province surrounding Milan. In 374 his Roman rhetoric proved its value when a dispute over episcopal succession arose in the local Christian church. The Arian bishop, Maxentius, had died, and the Arians were not happy with his likely replacement. To prevent the dispute from erupting into a riot, Ambrose began speaking to calm down the crowd. A voice shouted, "Ambrose, bishop." Soon the entire group joined the chant. In a week, Ambrose went from catechumen to baptized Christian to consecrated bishop of Milan. The Arians also accepted the choice of the Nicene-adhering Ambrose because of his consideration and kindness in dealing with them.

Three years later, in 377, his sister, Marcellina, requested his advice on how to live out her decision to dedicate her life to Jesus as a single woman. She and other women, as well as young men, felt called to give themselves to God's service, in ways that did not include marriage. A new path was opening in the Church, and it needed guidelines. Although the call was recorded in Scripture, the path for living it was not. St. Matthew (19:11–12) describes celibacy and virginity as Jesus told the apostles: "Not all men can receive this precept, but only those to whom it is given. . . . He who is able to receive this, let him receive it." (RSVCE) St. Paul opened the door a bit further in 1 Cor 7:7–9: "I wish that all were as I myself am. But each has his own special gift from God, one of one kind and one of another."

In helping his hearers understand how to better live this "special gift from God," Ambrose called upon his own education in Roman culture and history, Greek mythology, and wisdom in the ways of the world. When he describes the challenges to living a chaste commitment, we see that the fourth century was no more of a Christian golden age than any other time. Sixty years after the Edict of Constantine gave the protection of the Roman Empire to Christian belief and practice, that same empire was falling into economic and political collapse even though its population was steadily being Christianized. To help his sister and others, he outlined a new theological framework which showed reason and purpose, virtues to acquire and apply to one's spiritual struggle, and an emphasis on prayer and the sacraments to persevere to the end of life. With his emphasis on struggle and the acquisition of virtue, it is no surprise that St. Ambrose coined the term "cardinal virtues" to describe the core virtues of prudence, justice, fortitude, and temperance.

With his admonitions on struggle and safeguarding their calling, Ambrose channels enthusiasm and desire into a path of sustainable dedication. His program unfolds in two ways. First, he defends and exalts the nobility and pre-eminence of the path chosen for the exclusive love of God rather than love through his creatures. Then, he attacks the false arguments of those who regard celibacy and chastity as a threat to the established order of society by illustrating the contradictions inherent in the half-pagan culture which surrounded the first Christians, and which influenced even Christian parents to oppose and persecute their children who sought God above marriage and traditional family life. He mocks the pagan idea of virginity, which was temporary only and hardly chaste, and he gives almost incredible accounts of opposition to those who sought nothing but to be left alone to imitate Christ. In reading these letters and homilies today, we see how much life has changed, and how much it remains the same whenever opposition or obstacles arise to those who decide to overcome the world to follow a life of holiness through dedication to God alone.

INTRODUCTION

I HAVE TRANSLATED[1] **HERE SOME SERMONS** preached by Saint Ambrose in Milan nearly sixteen centuries ago. In 377, three years after his episcopal consecration, he wrote out three *libri* of them, which he called *de virginibus,* at the request of his sister Marcellina, in Rome. A fourth *liber* is called in some manuscripts *de virginitate*; this title may not be authentic, and the book looks like a disjointed collection of notes from various sermons, but it may still be the authentic voice of Ambrose.

Saint Ambrose is an attractive personality. The biography by his follower Paulinus and Augustine's references to him in the *Confessions* portray a man of remarkable kindness. In 374 AD, he found himself propelled by popular will out of a distinguished administrative career and installed so rapidly as bishop of Milan that his baptism and consecration were separated by only a week. With a wonderful combination of strength and humility he abandoned all his official dignities and set about learning his new work. He read the Bible assiduously, though anyone at any time might interrupt his reading to seek his help or advice. One man to profit by such advice was Augustine himself.

With the Bible and prayer, Ambrose prepared himself for his main episcopal task, teaching. As bishop, he preached

1. The Latin text is in volume 16 of Migne's *Patrologia Latina.* There is a later recension by G. Salvati in the *Corona Patrum Salesiana,* and a fine critical edition by Ignatius Cazzaniga (*de virginibus* 1948; *de virginitate* 1964) in the Turin *Corpus Paravianum.* There is a very fine biography of the Saint in English: F. Holmes Dudden, *The Life and Times of Saint Ambrose* (2 vols. Oxford 1935).

every week during the liturgy, and in periods such as Lent, daily. His writings are the main record of these sermons, which were possibly transcribed in church. This makes them prolix, repetitive and unsystematic, but also spontaneous.

The idea of exclusive dedication to God had just caught the Latin half of Christendom. Athanasius preaching in Western exile, and Jerome newly returned from the desert near Antioch, had spread the ideal. Ambrose takes it up with unparalleled enthusiasm. All his ethical writings, except his work on clerical duties (*De officiis*), are devoted to the subject of virginity. They comprise the *De virginibus libri tres, De viduis, De virginitate, De institutionis virginis,* and the *Exhortatio virginitatis,* all based on sermons. Alongside these in the printed editions we usually find a hard-hitting little book called *De lapsu virginis;* this is probably not the work of Ambrose but of a contemporary bishop, Nicetas.

Ambrose's sermons must have been impressive. From his writings it appears that Milan girls were so taken by his preaching that their mothers began to fear for their worldly prospects and to keep them from going to church.

Ambrose also devoted attention to widows: either destitute elderly ladies who were maintained at Church expense, or single women devoted to works of charity. We have his little book of advice for these. He is our best early authority in the Western church on the ideals of the virgin. For example, recall what St. Jerome in 384 sent to one Eustochium (Epistle 22):

> If you wish to know how many vexations that the virgin avoids and how many the married woman runs into, read Tertullian's book to a philosopher friend (lost) and the splendid book by St. Cyprian (*de habitu Virginis*), and the compositions of Pope Damasus in prose and verse. Then there are the little pamphlets our own Ambrose recently

> wrote for his sister (*de Virginibus*). In these he has expressed himself very fully: in fact he has looked up, arranged, and written out everything relevant to the praise of virginity.

Ambrose made two main points: first, the virgin is the spouse of Christ; second, ideal Christianity means chastity and celibacy. The virgin's veil had much the same appearance as that of Roman married women; she is wedded to Christ. This wedding had been a main point already in Greek writings such as the *Dialogue* of Methodius, a much more stylish piece of literature than Ambrose's sermons.

But Ambrose takes up the idea with new zest and detail. He tells us a good deal about the ceremony of commitment, and we can see a strong parallel between it and the ordinary Roman marriage ceremony. He preserves the full text of a bishop's address on such occasions; the Bishop was Pope Liberius, before whom Ambrose's own sister was committing herself. One of Ambrose's own episcopal addresses for the occasion is given at the beginning of his book on her training (*De institutione virginis*), meant for one Ambrosia. After the address, he ends with a reference to the virginity of our Lady, which makes the work interesting as an early piece of Latin mariology.

The idea of the mystic wedding with Christ explains the rather striking severity pronounced against lapses. This and the attack on the (pagan) Vestal virgins seem the only points where Ambrose gives an impression of harshness. Bishop Nicetas considered a lapse from virginity as equivalent to adultery: Ambrose does not go this far, but he does think it a very serious offence against God. Virginity is to be guarded at all costs; he would even countenance suicide in its defence.

The idea of the virgin wedded to Christ makes him draw heavily on the Canticle (Song of Solomon) for his ideas. His

De virginitate is practically a phrase-by-phrase commentary on it. The picturesque detail of this love-song had been allegorized by the Jews as the union between Yahweh and his Chosen People, and in consequence, by Christians, as the union between Christ and the Church. The Greek Fathers repeated that the virgin, especially the Blessed Virgin, is the Church's ideal representative, and so Ambrose feels no difficulty in this new application of Solomon's song.

Virginity the nucleus of Christian virtue

Some of Ambrose's quotations from Scripture may not be literally accurate and the arguments based on them may appear naive from the point of view of modern interpretation. But we must credit him with the simple ideal of using the inspired book, in the best Latin translation available to him, as the handbook of his work of preaching a very definite and practical asceticism. It certainly lent appeal to his words. He was convinced that he would find no better vocabulary for his new episcopal task of preaching than the words Christ had used to describe himself and his mission. Christ was the Word of the Old Testament made flesh. From the Bible comes the core of all his arguments; the Incarnation is a brand-new Creation, with a new Adam and a new Eve; Christ and Mary are both virginal, as in Paradise before the Fall. The Christian who is committed to virginity shares that perfection and that paradise. So, virginity is the essential nucleus of Christian virtue. Sanctity is purity. All Ambrose's moral writings turn on this one theme.

Ambrose's interpretation of the Scripture in arguing this point is not arbitrary. It seems that he took his lines of thought from previous interpretation. We should expect as much from a Bishop new to his task but anxious to build up his supply of orthodox teaching, shunning heresy. No doubt he kept the Greek Fathers alongside his Bible.

In the monastic settlements of the Near East, the cradle of the ideal, there were then numerous sorts of ascetic: solitary, semi solitary, cenobite. In Milan, the task was to live that life of the desert in her own home, meeting her colleagues only in church. Bologna witnesses some banding together into a community; the same thing happens in Jerome's foundation at Bethlehem. It is the bishop's duty, says Ambrose, to see if the woman's home is likely to nourish her asceticism. The home has to be a genuine pattern of the desert. The main rule is silence; the nun must have words for none but Christ, her Lover (*de virginitate* 80). Even in Church she is warned not to speak except in the liturgical responses; obviously the Church-going women of the time were much given to chattering (*De virginibus* 3.11–13). These specially-dedicated women seem to have occupied a special place apart in the church and to have received the *osculum pacis* (kiss of peace) before the rest of the congregation, and then bestowed it on lay women. The sermon addressed to these dedicated souls was heard of course by everybody and contained the odd suitable point for the benefit of fathers or mothers.

We gather some detail about dress. The veil was probably the sort worn by other married women and there may not have been much other distinction. Ambrose is at pains to condemn all attempts at cosmetics or hairstyles. We hear a good deal about prayer. He insists on fixed hours, obviously on a liturgical pattern, "seven times a day" (*De virginibus* 3, 18–19; *De instit.* 8–9). Prayer in practice means the psalter, interspersed with the Lord's Prayer. Praise always gets first place, before supplication.

This fervent life came under strong criticism in the Roman world. Cultivated pagans could see no point in people running away from social obligations and family ties, depleting the imperial services and reducing the growth of population. Ambrose devotes much space to refuting such attacks, both pagan and Christian. He could find no interruption of ordinary life and no depletion of the imperial population. Besides, his balance of view is shown by the praise he is careful to bestow on marriage. He stresses that marriage is good and sacramental. But virginity is the greater good, the more perfect state. It alone is ideal Christianity, and so, following the examples of Christ, Christ's mother, and the martyrs, the profession of virginity is the very best act a human being can perform (*De virginibus* 1, 10–11).

James Shiel
May 1963

ART Collection / Alamy Stock Photo

Wikimedia Commons

Above: Ambrose restrained the emperor Theodosius (347–395) from entering Milan cathedral for not doing public penance after an intemperate response to the killing of a Roman general in Greece, which led to the massacre of 7,000 in Thessalonica.

Right: Ambrose described St. Agnes as "not old enough for torture, but quite mature in her victory over it." She became a model for those who would endure any trial for the sake of giving themselves to Christ.

Peter Horree / Alamy Stock Photo

Legend describes a swarm of bees landing on the face of the infant Ambrose, a foretelling of his future eloquence.

Web Gallery of Art / Wikimedia Commons

Ambrose (on right) baptized Augustine in Milan at Easter in the year 387. Augustine would become the Church's first moral theologian.

DE VIRGINIBUS

THE FIRST BOOK

1. Word has reached us from heaven that we shall have to account for every profitless thing we say (Mt 12:36). The servant who is given his talents, his coins of spiritual grace, and instead of soundly investing them hides them in the ground, either through lack of enterprise or through greed, will most certainly get into trouble when his master returns (Mt 25:14). My own talents are small. But I still have the duty of investing the divine word in the minds of the people and I am afraid of the day when I shall be asked to show the accrued return. I am more afraid because the Lord is going to look for effort rather than effect. That is why I have now decided to try my pen. Writing will cause me less shame than speaking: a book can't blush.

2. I have little brainpower to rely on, but I am encouraged by instances of God's kindness. Balaam's ass was granted speech when God so willed (Num 22:28). If that angel comes and stands by me with all my packsaddle of worldly cares, I shall be able to open the lips that have been closed for so long. He can free me from the bond of my ignorance as he freed the ass from that of nature. In the Ark of the Covenant, Aaron's rod blossomed (Num 17:8); in the Church, God may just as easily bring flowers from my knotty branches. If he spoke through the thorns of the burning bush (Ex 3:4), may we not expect him to speak through a human being? He did not despise that bush, so I hope he will also shine through my thorns. Perhaps some people will wonder at the light shining amid my branches, a lighted bush that will not burn them. At

the sound of my voice, some will, like Moses, take off their shoes; I mean to say, they will free the march of their mind from bodily encumbrance.

The burning bush as a symbol of purity

3. Of course that sort of miracle happens only to holy people. But here am I lying under a fig-tree that is still barren. I wish Jesus would come and look at me (Jn 1:48). If he did, my tree would bear fruit even after my three fruitless years. Or is that too big a hope for a sinner? At least, then, perhaps the vinedresser mentioned in the Gospel will give my tree another year until he digs round it and gives it its basket of manure—though he may have already got his orders to cut it down (Lk 13:6). So doing he may well raise the weak from the earth, the poor from the dunghill. Those are happy men who tie their horses under the vine or the olive (cf. Gen 49:11), devoting the hours of their work to the joy of the sunlight. I am still under the shade of my fig tree; in other words, I am under the enticement of worldly delight, a type of tree that is too stunted, too brittle, too tender, to be of any use.

4. It may astonish you that I start writing when you know my word-power is so poor. Well, let us open the Gospels and see what happened to the priests there. The prophet Zachary is proof that pen may write where tongue fails (Lk 1:63). If writing the name John gave that dumb man back his speech, maybe I, however tongue-tied, may get the gift of words by writing of Christ? Mind you, the saying of the Prophet is: "His birth is beyond our knowing" (Is 53:8) It is only as his poor household slave that I can venture to speak of his family. The Lord most pure has established a family of his own here on earth amid all our bodily weakness.

5. It fits us nicely that today is the feast of a virgin, and so my sermon in church must be on virginity. With some of that sermon I can start my book. The feast of a virgin teaches us to pursue purity; that of a martyr to offer sacrifices. It is the feast of Saint Agnes. Men, admire her. Children, take courage. Wives, be dumbfounded. Girls, imitate her. How can I add anything to her glory when even the etymology of her name—in Greek it means "pure"—glows with her praise? Since her pure constancy was beyond her years, her pure virtue beyond her nature, I think that name of hers was not just a human one but an oracle foretelling her martyrdom.

6. Actually my sermon is helped by the fact that her name is such a title of purity. I shall simply call upon this martyr to praise her virginity. The best panegyric is the one that has not to be searched for, being ready at hand and demanding no cleverness, no eloquence. One little word is enough: Agnes. Old men, young men, little children, can chant it. The highest possible praise is what comes from everybody, and everybody can preach the panegyric of this martyr: they need only mention her name.

7. She was said to be a martyr at twelve. It was hideous cruelty which did not spare such tender years. But faith looks even more powerful when it finds its witness in one of such tender age. Scarcely did the deathblow find room on her tiny body. But though tinier than the sword, she still conquered the sword. Normally, little girls of that age can hardly bear a harsh look from their parents; they shrink from the prick of a pin as if it were a battle wound. Agnes was not afraid of the cruel hands of the executioners. She was not terrified by the clanking of prison chains. She freely offered her body to the lance of the raging soldier, knowing nothing of death but still

prepared to face it. When dragged before the pagan altars she had no hesitation in extending her hands amid the flames, praying to Christ and in that place of sacrilegious fire making Christ's victorious sign of the cross. She put her own hands and head into the irons even though those tiny limbs were too small for them. Surely, a new sort of martyrdom.

The victorious Agnes

8. Not old enough for torture, but quite mature in her victory over it; too young to fight but still able to win; an expert in virtue despite her age. No bride would go off so full of joy to her honeymoon as she went to torture; she hurried along. Her hairstyle proclaimed Christ: not the usual plaits but the virgin's close crop, garlanded with virtues instead of flowers. Everyone else cried but her eyes were dry. Many wondered why she was so spendthrift with a life which she had barely tasted; here she was, giving it away as if she were at the end of it. All were amazed that she should be a witness to the divine before she could yet witness her own humanity. Naturally then, people believed that she must have received from God what could not come from man; what is beyond nature can only come from the Author of nature.

9. Her executioner used every threat to deter her, every blandishment to dissuade her from her resolve. Many desired to have her in marriage. She simply said: "It is an insult to my spouse to think of giving pleasure to another. He who chose me first shall always possess me. Man with the axe, what is holding you up? I want this body to die rather than be admired by eyes I do not desire." She stood in prayer and then bowed her neck. One could see the tough executioner trembling as if he himself were condemned. His hand shook and his face went pale at her danger, though she herself had no

fears at all. In that one victim you see a double martyrdom, a bearing-of-witness to both modesty and faith; she held on to her virginity and gained the martyr's crown as well.

10. I now go on to speak of virginity. Love of purity prompts me, and the claims of your own silent holiness, my dear sister (Marcelina). Virginity is not the sort of subject to be just touched upon in passing, for it is a primary virtue. Virginity is not praiseworthy just because it is found in martyrs like Agnes, but because it makes martyrs.

11. The human mind finds virginity difficult to understand for it does not fall within the norms of nature. The natural powers of speech will not express it for it is above the merely natural. It has carried down from heaven something to imitate on earth. Virginity quite rightly looks to heaven for its manner of life for there is the virgin's spouse. By-passing the clouds, the sky, the angels, the stars, virginity discovered the Word of God in the bosom of the Father and received wholeheartedly therefrom. For who could find such a wealth of goodness and leave it behind? "Thy very name soothes the heart like flow of oil; what wonder the maids should love thee." (Song 1:1). I did not invent the idea that those who will neither marry nor be given in marriage will be as the angels in heaven (Mt 22:30). Small wonder that they are compared to angels when they are wedded to the Lord of angels. No one can deny that this way of life descended from heaven for it was not to be found on earth until God came down and put on human limbs. Only when the Virgin conceived, and the Word was made flesh, could flesh think of becoming God.

12. Someone, of course, may remind me that Elias was free from all bodily desire. Yes, and so he was taken up to heaven in a chariot (2 Kings 2:11) and appeared with our Lord in

glory (Mt 17:3) and is the precursor of the second coming (Mal 4:5). Mary, also, the sister of Aaron, took a tambourine and with virginal modesty led the dances (Ex 15:20). But she was an image of the Church which, being virginal in spirit, has gathered her holy multitudes together to chant the divine songs, like those chosen virgins who were in the temple of Jerusalem. Notice what Paul says: "When all this happened to them it was symbol of things to come." (1 Cor 10:11). The symbols involved only a few persons, but the reality signified is for large numbers.

13. For when the Lord entered this human frame of ours, he linked together divinity and humanity in one dwelling without incurring any taint in the mingling, and then his heavenly way of living spread throughout the world in human bodies. So, we have that new race which the angels who ministered to him on earth (Mt 4:11) foretold, a race which would serve the Lord with the ministry of a pure body. This is the heavenly army on earth promised by a host of angels chanting praise. We may conclude then, that though we have ancient precedent for virginity, the fullness of its profession comes from Christ.

Contrast with pagan models

14. What I speak of is not possessed also by the pagans; it is not found among the barbarians; nor among the animals. All these, of course, breathe the same air as we do, have the same bodily state as ourselves, have similar processes of reproduction. In virginity, however, Christians do not admit the reproach of similarity. Virginity is, admittedly, professed by the pagans, but they have no hesitation in violating its consecration. It gets no respect of any kind from the barbarians, and of course it is unknown in the animal world.

15. In this connection it is no good pointing out to me the Vestal virgins and the priests of Pallas. Their chastity is not measured by habit but only by time. It is prescribed for a limited period, not forever. That is a very lax sort of integrity which has corruption in store for a later stage of life. By setting a fixed time-limit they imply that the virgins must not and cannot persevere. A very strange sort of religion, this, where young women are ordered to be chaste and old ones to be shameless! Perhaps chaste is the wrong word, for this chastity of theirs is but the restraint of law; a woman can hardly be called chaste when the law can dismiss her virtue. What strange sacraments and virtues, in the one moment imposing a law for chastity and granting a licence for vice! A woman is not chaste by force or by hire. Nor is modesty compatible with being daily exposed to vicious eyes, scourged by their sinful gaze. The Vestals enjoy state immunities and cash rewards; this, I think, is the worst aspect of their laxity, putting their chastity up for sale. They get their price for keeping it and they get their price for losing it; its market value can always be assessed. The woman of course who sells can never buy back again.

16. I need say nothing about the pagan cult of the mother-goddess, Cybele, with whose votaries uncleanness has the place of a regular discipline; and I wish it were confined to women only. Shall I go on to talk of the orgies of the Wine God, where religious ceremony is just an incitement to desire? There the priest's life can hardly be very sublime, for it is to the actual crimes of the gods that he pays reverence. Such ceremony of course has no need for consecrated virginity.

17. Let us see if the rules of philosophy ever resulted in virginity. Remember that philosophy claims to be the teacher of all virtues. Well, there is that famous story of a virgin from

the sect of the philosopher Pythagoras. A tyrant was forcing her to divulge a secret, and to prevent herself from yielding to torture she bit off her tongue and spat it in his face. From then on his interrogation could find no reply.

18. That was a girl of brave mind, but her body was not so brave. Though exemplary in her silence her chastity was but a shadow. She could not be bested by torture, but she was unequal to the attacks of passion. She could hide the secrets of her mind but not the desire of her body. She was able to conquer nature; yet she was incapable of self-restraint. If only her modesty had resided in her voice! But maybe her suffering was all to the end of hushing her guilt. We can hardly call her a winner on all scores: the tyrant was unable to secure what he sought, but only too able to secure what he had not sought.

Different courage

19. Our virgins have a finer bravery than hers. They can overcome even the powers that are invisible. Their victory is not just over flesh and blood, but over the prince of this world, the ruler of this age. Agnes was younger than that girl but far greater in virtue; her victory was far more splendid, her fortitude more steadfast. She did not cut off her tongue through fear; she preserved it to proclaim her victory. She had nothing to fear disclosing, for her confession was not of guilt but of faith. That Pythagorean virgin merely hid a secret, but Agnes revealed her praise of the Lord. Her years were not yet fit to confess him, but her character was.

20. In panegyrics it is usual to praise your subject's native land and parents, for by praising the ancestors you praise the descendants. Here I am not praising virginity, but giving examples which express it. Still, I now feel I ought to mention

its fatherland and parentage. Its fatherland first. If native place is taken to be where the ancestral home is, then the fatherland of chastity is heaven. There it is native but down here it is a stranger and wayfarer.

21. Virginal chastity is integrity without stain. Who else, then, can be its author but the stainless Son of God whose flesh saw no corruption, whose divinity knew no fault? From him you may gauge the merit of virginity. Christ was born of a virgin, even though he had existed before her from eternity. He was born of the Father before all ages but was born of the Virgin to redeem the ages; one birth is his by nature, the other he undertook for our benefit. One existed always, the other he willed in time.

22. Another merit of virginity: Christ is a virgin's spouse. To put it better, virginal chastity is espoused to him (for virginity belongs to Christ, not Christ to virginity). So, his bride, the Church, is a virgin. As virgin she has carried us in her womb, brought us forth, nourished us. Of her we read: "Where were ever such deeds heard of? Shall the snows of Lebanon melt from those wild peaks, shall they be dried up at their source, those icy torrents that flow down from it?"[1] Who is this virgin who drinks of the fountains of the Trinity, for whom water flows from the rock, for whom the udders remain full and honey flows? According to the Apostle the rock means Christ. Christ's nourishment does not fail; nor God's snowy brightness; nor the Spirit's stream of water. This is the Triad which nourishes the Church: Father and Son and Spirit.

23. From this mother, the Church, let us pass on to her daughters. "About virgins," says the Apostle, "I have no command from the Lord" (1 Cor 7:25 ff.). If this teacher

1. Jer 18:13 (but Ambrose follows a pre-Vulgate Latin version).

of nations has none, who else is likely to have? He did not have a command, but he did have an example. Virginity, in fact, cannot be imposed by law; it can only be desired, for the things that are above our nature are objects of desire and not of command. He goes on, then: "I would have you free from concern. He who is unmarried is concerned with God's claim, asking how he is to please God. A virgin is concerned with the Lord's claim, intent on holiness of body and spirit; whereas the married woman is concerned with the world's claim, asking how she is to please her husband."

24. I am not speaking against matrimony; I am only setting out the advantages of virginity. "He that is weak must be content with vegetable fare" (Rom 14:2). What I command is one thing, what I commend is another. "Art thou yoked to a wife? Then do not go about to free thyself. Art thou free of wedlock? Then do not go about to find a wife" (1 Cor 7:27). This is the command he gives for the married. And what does he say for the unwedded? "A man is well advised to give his ward in marriage, and still better advised not to give her in marriage" (1 Cor 7:38). The girl who marries does not sin by marrying; but the one who renounces marriage is a virgin for eternity. On the one hand you have a remedy for human infirmity, on the other the splendor of chastity. One state is not rebuked because the other is praised.

Benefits compared

25. Let us compare the benefits of wives with even the smallest of those enjoyed by virgins. A lady of rank may boast of her abundant offspring, but the more her children the more her labors. She may count her sons as so many consolations, but she ought to count them as troubles too. She weds to weep. Why these desires that end in tears? Her ambition leads

her to conception and pregnancy, and her sorrow appears on the scene long before its reward. She must face the illness of childbearing. Motherhood begins in danger, ends in danger, and brings sorrow sooner than pleasure. It is purchased with perils, and it does not come just as you want it.

26. No need have I to dwell on the troubles of rearing children, of educating them, of marrying them off. Even happy mothers must face these troubles. As posterity increases, so do anxieties. I must not pursue this topic: it would alarm the ears of too many good parents. You can see, dear sister, how bad these troubles are when it is safer not to mention them. They are of the present only. But a time is coming when men will say: "It is well for the barren, for the wombs that never bore children." (Lk 23:29). The children of this world are born and in turn give birth, but the daughter of the Kingdom abstains from all pleasure of sex that she may be holy in body and spirit.

27. There is no need for me to go over the menial ministrations and servilities women must show towards their men. Service was allotted to them by God even before it was allotted to their slaves (Gen 3:16). I mention this that they may obey even more willingly. If they are holy it earns for them the reward of charity; if they are sinners, it provides a penalty for sin. But here there arise such incentives to sin as the use of make-up, through fear of not being able to please husbands.[2]

28. Defacing the countenance is an easy way to defacing virtue. How silly, changing the reality of nature to produce a mere travesty of it, respecting their husbands' judgment while forfeiting their own! A woman who thus alters the face

2. See St. Augustine, *De Doctrina Christo*, Chapter 4, 21.

she was born with has obviously been passing judgment on herself; contriving to please another means being displeased with herself. Lady, we cannot get a truer verdict upon your lack of beauty than your own efforts at concealment. If you are really pretty, why try to hide (it)? And if you are ugly, why make a pretence of being pretty? You are going to derive no benefit either from your own consciousness or from another's delusion. It is a substitute woman you are training him to admire; it is another you are trying to please. It will be pointless getting annoyed when he abandons you for somebody else; you are already teaching him a sort of adultery even as regards your own person. You are, I fear, the cause of your own misfortune. The very woman of the streets detests being a procurer even though she herself has employed one; however cheap she is she likes to sin to her own profit and not to another's. Adultery is almost preferable to sinning against oneself, for though in the one case modesty goes by the board in the other nature herself goes too.

29. It is a costly business for even a handsome woman to avoid displeasing her men. Above, expensive necklaces; below, an embroidered dress trailing on the ground. One wonders whether beauty is provided by nature or by the shop. Perfumes are a further allurement, ears must carry their cargo of rings, and even the color of the eyes must be changed. With so many borrowed items, how much of the ensemble is actual woman? The fact is that she has lost her senses, imagining she can live without them.

30. You, virgins, are lucky not to know such ornaments—"torments "would be a better word. Holy modesty is your makeup, and chastity is your finery. Not depending on human eyes, you do not base your attractions on their

delusion. You have, of course, your own battle for beauty but it is the beauty of virtue, not that of the body. This beauty time cannot wither, nor death remove, nor sickness impair. The only judge you seek to please is God, who can appreciate beauty of soul even in an imperfect body. You, virgins, know no pain of pregnancy or childbirth; yet you have your numerous offspring, for the chaste soul has everyone for her child. Assured of descendants, she knows no bereavement and always has heirs.

31. And so the Church is virginal in her espousals and yet fruitful in children. She is virgin and mother. She brought us into life, conceived not of man but of the Spirit, in a birth free from bodily pain and full of the joy of the angels. Her nourishment is not the milk of the body but that with which the Apostle nurtured the tender infancy of Christ's flock (1 Cor 3:1). What married woman can boast of a family to compare with that of the Church, virgin-pure in her sacraments, mother of her peoples? The Scripture attests that motherhood: "She is to have more children now, the Lord says, than wife whose husband remains with her" (Is 54:1). The Church is without husband, but she is not without spouse, for in the whole body of believers, as well as in the individual soul, she takes as eternal spouse the Word of God, in a union free of shame or loss and fruitful in the spirit.

Virtues to teach the young

32. Parents, you have now heard the virtues to teach your daughters, the disciplines in which to instruct them. The outcome will be that their merit will remove your sins. Remember that a virgin is your gift to God, a parental offering, a pure act of priesthood. A virgin is a victim sacrificed by her mother, and by that daily act of sacrifice the divine anger

is appeased. The virgin is also pledged without loss to her parents: she will not worry them for a dowry or leave them deserted at home or offend them by evildoing.

33. Some men desire grandchildren and the ultimate honor of being grandfathers. This means giving up their own children in favor of a stranger, giving up family that is certain to pursue what is an uncertain hope. So, they give away all their possessions and may very well be asked to give even more. If a man fails to pay his daughter's dowry on demand it may be wrenched from him by force. Should he survive to old age he is nothing but a burden. This shows that a son-in-law is not a free acquisition but has to be bought; and he in turn has his own duty of selling your daughter's qualities to his parents. Just think: was she carried in the womb all those weary months to be handed over now to another? Was all your care over her upbringing just to have her taken away the more quickly?

34. But somebody is going to ask me: Are you then against the idea of marrying? No, I am in favor of it, and I will oppose anybody who condemns it. Indeed, I am in the habit of recounting, as examples of singular virtue, the marriages of Sara and Rebecca and Rachel and the other women of old. He who condemns marriage condemns children, condemns in fact the survival of all human society. How could humanity continue at all from age to age unless the attraction of wedlock induced people to procreate children? I could never start preaching about the pure Isaac going to the altar as victim of his father's piety (Gen 22:2), or about Jacob, though still in a human body, seeing God and bestowing his new name, Israel, upon his people (Gen 32:27). I could never mention them if I condemned marriage, in which they had their origin. Evil men have an argument with which the wise

may heartily agree; by condemning marriage they declare that they themselves ought never to have been born!

35. No, I am not against marriage. I am only recounting the benefits of consecrated virginity, which is a thing for the few while marriage will always be for the many. Virginity cannot do without its source, and that source is marriage. I am really comparing something that is good with something else that is good: special excellences come to light that way. In all this I am not just giving an opinion of my own but repeating what the Holy Spirit said through the Prophet: "How fair is the childless life that is nobly lived" (Wis 4:1).

36. Girls about to marry boast of the good looks of their loved ones, but in this they cannot compare with those who have professed virginity and can say: "Thine is more than mortal beauty; thy lips overflow with gracious utterance" (Ps 45:2–4). This Spouse of theirs is not given over to worthless pursuits, and is not puffed up by riches that vanish, for his throne endures for ever. "The daughters of kings come out to meet thee; at thy right hand stands the queen in Ophir gold arrayed. Listen, my daughter, and consider my words attentively: thou art to forget henceforth thy own nation and the house of thy father; thy beauty now is all for the king's delight; he is thy Lord and worship belongs to him" (Ps 45:9–10).

Interior beauty

37. Notice how the Holy Spirit, as witnessed by his divine writing, has assigned to you royalty and gold and beauty. You have royalty because you are the spouse of an everlasting king; you hold your soul unconquered and, no captive to the allurements of pleasure, you reign as a queen. You have gold too. This metal when tried by fire becomes even more

precious; so, the virgin's body when consecrated to the Spirit increases its splendor. As for beauty, who can imagine greater beauty than her who is loved by the divine King, approved by the divine Judge, possessed by God, and consecrated to him? Ever the happy fiancée, ever unwedded, she can know no end of love and her virginity can suffer no loss.

38. It is, surely, genuine beauty, lacking nothing, which can hear from the Lord: "Fair in every part, my true love, no fault in all thy fashioning! Venture forth from Lebanon and come to me, my bride, my queen that shall be! Leave Amana behind thee, Sanir and Hermon heights, where the lairs of lions are, where the leopards roam the hills" (Song 4:7–8). These phrases show the perfect and faultless beauty of the virginal soul, which, consecrated at God's altars, unbent by mortal fears even amid the assaults and deceits of evil spirits, ever intent on the mysteries of God, wins a spouse whose heart teems with joy. "Wine," says the Psalmist, "will rejoice man's heart" (Ps 103:15).

39. "No spices," says the Song, "can match the perfume that breathes from thy garments" (Song 4:10). Later: "The perfume of thy garments is as trees of Lebanon." (Song 4:11). We notice a grading here. That first perfume excels the spices which were used in the Savior's burial; their fragrance is a sign that the body's movements are dead, the delights of its members departed. The second perfume is like the incense of Lebanon and betrays the incorruptibility of the Lord's body, virginal chastity's noblest flower.

40. Let your works be "as honey dripping from the comb" (Song 2:1). Your virginity stands comparison with the bees. It is industrious, modest, continent. The bee feeds on the dew, knows no sexual intercourse, produces honey. The food of the virgin is the divine Word which descends like dew.

Virginal modesty knows no violation. The lips of the virgin produce no bitterness but words of sweetness. The virgin's labor is shared with others, and so is its fruit.

41. I should like you, my daughter, to imitate the tiny bee which feeds on the flowers and from them collects and forms its offspring. My daughter, copy that bee. Your words must have no deceit, no untruth; they must be the honey of simplicity and dignity.

42. Let your lips generate the lasting posterity of your merits. Gather not just for yourself but for many others. How do you know when your soul may be required from you? You do not want to leave behind your granary bins heaped full of corn that no longer serve your life or its merits when you are snatched away to where you cannot convey your treasures. Your riches, then, must be for the poor. Since they share the same nature as yourself let them also share your possessions.

43. Also, I want to point out to you a flower that is worth the picking, him who said: "Count me as the wild rose on the lowland plain, wild lily on the mountain slopes, a lily among the branches" (Song 2:1). This is a clear indication that virtues are surrounded by the spiritual brambles of vice and that nobody can gather their fruit unless he goes about it cautiously.

44. Spread your spiritual wings and fly over those vices if you wish to reach Christ, "so high above us all, that stoops to regard both heaven and earth" (Ps 112:5). Like the cedar of Lebanon which has its top in the clouds and its roots in the earth, Christ's divine origin is in heaven, but his humanity is on earth and produces there celestial fruit. Search diligently for such a precious blossom; you will find it only in the valley of your own heart, for its perfume is best perceived by the lowly.

45. He loves to grow in those gardens where Susanna found him on her walk, she who was ready to die rather than be dishonored (Dan 13:7). He himself describes that garden: "My bride, my true love, a close garden; hedged all about, a spring shut in and sealed." (Song 4:12). That spring of pure water has the image of God stamped on its seal and the coming and going of spiritual beasts will not pollute the stream. There modesty is ever enclosed by a wall of the spirit and is not open to rapine. Inaccessible to thieves, the garden is redolent of the vine and the olive and is bright with the rose. Piety grows like the vine, peace like the olive, virginal modesty like the rose. Such fragrance was on the garments of the patriarch Jacob when he heard the words: "How it breathes about this son of mine, the fragrance of earth when the Lord's blessing is on it." (Gen 27:27). The harvest of the holy patriarch's field was fruit garnered after hard labor, whereas virginity is the land of blossoms.

Advice to be faithful

46. Gird yourself, virgin, and if you want a garden like this to breathe its fragrance upon you, fence it in with the rules of the prophets. Set a guard on your mouth, post a sentry before your lips (Ps 140:3), so that you may be able to say: "An apple-tree in the wild woodland, shade cool to rest under, fruit sweet to the taste, such is he my heart longs for matched with his fellows" (Song 2:3). "I found him, so tenderly loved, and now that he is mine, I will never leave him, never let him go" (Song 3:5). "Into his garden, then, let my true love come and taste his fruit" (Song 5:1). "Come with me, my true love; for us the country ways" (Song 7:11). "My sweetheart? Among ten thousand you shall know him, so white is the color of his fashioning and so red" (Song 5:10). It is only right that

you should know well the one you love. You must be able to recognize in him the whole mystery of godhead innate and manhood assumed. In the Song the word "white" denotes the splendor of the Father, and "red" the flesh born of the Virgin. In him the colors of both natures shine radiantly. Remember, however, that the white mark of divinity is older than the red sacramental sign of his humanity. His birth from the Virgin was not his first beginning; it was a coming to her from his previous state of divinity.

47. He was racked by the soldiers and pierced by a lance that he might heal us by the blood of his holy wound. Being meek and lowly of heart, kindly in appearance, his words to you will surely be: "North wind, awake; wind of the south, awake and come; blow through this garden of mine and set its fragrance all astir" (Song 4:16). To all points of the world the breeze of sacred fervor has blown and the virginity of mortal limbs has given its fragrance. "Fair art thou and graceful, my heart's love; for beauty Jerusalem itself is not thy match" (Song 6:3). Your beauty is not just that of the body which is victim to disease and old age. The glory of the virgin, her good repute and merit, cannot be upset by accident or death.

48. As you are not at all to be compared with the citizens of earth but with those of heaven, whose life you live here, take your orders from your Lord, who says: "Hold me close to thy heart, close as locket or bracelet fits" (Song 8:6). Like the imprint of a seal must be your wisdom and deeds, in which the imprint of Christ, the equal of God the Father, is to shine and reveal all the divinity taken from the Father. That is why Paul talks about the seal set on our faith by the gift of the Spirit (Eph 1:13), for we have the Father's image in the Son and we have the seal of the Son in the Spirit. Stamped thus with the Trinity we must be careful not to let levity of habits

or the deceit of any bad action break the seal on our hearts. Not that you have any need for undue fear.

49. To virgins the Church gives ample protection. Guarding her tender offspring she rises like "a fortress with turrets" (Song 8:10). Breaking the attack of the enemy she wins peace for her children in her stronghold of maternal bravery. So the Prophet says: "Let there be peace within thy ramparts, ease in thy strongholds" (Ps 121:7).

50. Stronger protections still, the Lord of peace himself cherishes his vineyard and watches its branches multiply. His attention commands and tempers the breezes to the growing fruits, as he himself says: "A vineyard I have, of my own, here at my side; keep thy thousand pieces, Solomon, and let each vine-dresser have his two hundred; not mine to grudge them" (Song 8:12).

Chastity made the angels

51. Or, as we read further back: "Sixty warriors to guard, none braver in Israel; swordsmen all well trained for battle" (Song 3:7–8). The greater the fruit, the greater the defence; the holier one is, the greater his security. So Eliseus the prophet said that hosts of angels were his protection (2 Kings 6:17). Joshua had sight of the leader of the heavenly army (Josh 5:14). They who can fight for us are able to guard our fruits. There is a special bodyguard for you, holy virgins, whose inviolate purity keeps the Lord's couch holy. No wonder that angels fight for you whose own warfare is angelic in character. Virginity deserves the protection of those whose life it shares.

52. I need say no more in its praise. Chastity made the angels, for he who preserved it is an angel, he who lost it is a devil. Hence religion borrowed the title: the religion of the

true God is called a virgin, but that which makes false gods is called a harlot. Then there is the resurrection, pledge of which you already hold. "When the dead rise again," says Christ, "there is no marrying and giving in marriage; they are as the angels in heaven." (Mt 22:30). What is a promise for the rest of us is already a reality for you; you have possession, we have only desire. You are in this world but not of it. The world could have had use for you, but it lost its hold on you.

53. How remarkable that the angels fell from heaven to earth because of their intemperance, while virgins through their purity pass from earth to heaven. Happy are these virgins, tempted by no enticement of the body, debased by no corruption of the will. Food of frugality, drink of abstinence, keep them from knowing vice, keep them from knowing even the occasion of vice. Occasions of sin have often deceived even the just. Remember how the people of God sat down to eat and drink and then denied God (Ex 32:6). Lot, drunk and unaware, suffered the violent act of his own daughters (Gen 19:33). The two sons of Noah, turning away their faces, covered the nakedness of their father. The eldest son had shamelessly looked upon him, but the others, modest and dutiful, blushed, and covered him, deeming it wrong even to glance at him (Gen 9:22). Wine is powerful: it succeeded in denuding Noah, though the deluge had failed to do so.

Scorn for fashion

54. You are very lucky that no greed inflames you. The beggar asks for what you have, but if you have nothing he passes you by. The fruit of your labor is treasure for the needy. Even if it all amounts to only two coins, these are still matter for great generosity. Your poverty, my sister, frees you from great troubles. To tell you what you ought to avoid is not mine to teach

nor yours to learn. Perfect virtue needs no teacher; rather it provides one. You see that the woman who decks herself out to please is like one of those triumphal litters carried in the procession and drawing everybody's attention. But the more she tries to make a pleasing display the more she admits her ugliness; she displeases many in her effort to please one. Your very neglect of appearance is more effective; your lack of adornment is your beauty.

55. Look at those ears lacerated with piercings; pity that neck bent down under its load. Such penalties are not reduced by the precious quality of the stones. A chain round the neck or a fetter on the feet: be they iron or gold, neck is bowed and feet are hampered by them. Expense brings nothing to you women except the fear that those burdens may be taken from you, penalties which are not lightened by being inflicted upon you by your own sentence rather than another's. You are worse off than those condemned in court, for they wish to escape but you prefer to stay chained.

56. How wretched it is that a woman wanting to marry has practically to put herself up for sale like a slave and the highest bidder gets her. Slaves really are in a better position for often they can choose their masters. If a girl does her own choosing she is criticized; if she does not she is despised. However pretty and good she is, she at once fears and desires to be seen: she desires, for she wants to sell well; she fears, for she may not look nice enough. Her desires may be mocked and her fears may be realized in the suiting: a poor man may deceive her, a rich one grow tired of her, a handsome fellow laugh at her, a noble despise her.

57. Someone may remark: "You keep on chanting the praises of virginity to us day after day." Yes, I do go on saying the same things, but I fail to persuade my hearers. However,

that is not my fault. Postulants come from elsewhere to take their veil here, all the way from Piacenza, from Bologna, even from Morocco. It is rather a miracle: I talk here, my words act somewhere else. Perhaps I ought to do my preaching elsewhere to have the right effect here.

58. It seems that those who don't hear me can follow me, while those who do hear me fail. I have known several girls who were well disposed to my words but they were prevented from coming here by their mothers, and what is worse, by mothers who were widows. These I now address. If your daughters wanted to love a man, the law would allow them to choose the one they loved. If they may choose man, why not let them choose God?

59. See how sweet the fruit of modesty is when it has taken root in the affections of foreigners. From the distant parts of Morocco young women come here for their profession. Over there, their families are in the bonds of slavery, but innocence knows no captivity and even when suffering the lot of slavery it professes an eternal royalty.[3]

60. What shall I say of Bologna, a fine army of modesty, who renounce the delights of the world to inhabit virginity's sanctuary? They have left the company of men and the protection of parents. Their number is close on twenty (their fruit a hundred-fold), and in the battlements of Christ they are untiring soldiers of chastity. They sing their spiritual chants. With their own hands they earn their living and provide generous support for the poor.

61. Once the scent of hidden chastity comes their way they show themselves first-rate hunters; they track their prey right

3. St. Augustine, *Contra Pelagius*, 2.83; ep. 87.8; Ammian 28.

to its lair. If a choice bird is raised, up they all go in full flight after her, flapping their wings and calling loudly. Their one aim is to surround their prey in a community chorus until she is enticed into their gleaming company and, leaving home, falls into their snare.

Advice to parents

62. Parents do well to breathe upon their daughter the desire of purity. But it is even better when the fire of tender age takes no fuel from elders and of itself bursts into a blaze of chastity. Parents may then refuse a dowry; but remember, virgin, that your spouse is wealthy and, content with his riches, you need not look for the profits of your family. Virginal poverty is far more precious than the dowry account book.

63. Anyway, what girl have you heard was ever excluded from her legal inheritance simply because she opted for chastity? Parents may oppose her, but they secretly want her to win. They resist at first because they hesitate to believe her. They often flare up, to teach you to fight your way. They threaten to disown you to see if you are able to disregard the loss of worldly goods. They flatter you with exquisite enticements to see if the lure and variety of pleasure can soften your resolve. You are being drilled, virgin, all this time they are opposing you, and your first battles will be against these anxious desires of your parents. Girl, overcome at once your filial sentiments. If you can conquer the ties of home you can conquer the world.

64. Supposing you do lose your intended inheritance, the riches of heaven will surely compensate you for the loss of the perishable and flimsy goods of this world. If we trust the words of heaven, "none who leaves house or parents or brothers or wife or sons for the kingdom of God who will

not receive seven times as much in this life; and in the life to come he will have life everlasting" (see Mt 19:29). Let God be your trust; if you can trust your riches to men why not lend at interest to Christ? He is a safe keeper of your deposited hope and will pay out the coin of your faith at multiple interest. Truth does not lie, justice does not defraud, virtue does not deceive. But if all this does not convince you let us look at some actual examples.

What happens to those who opposed children's vocations

65. I once knew a girl who belonged to this world's nobility, though now she is among the nobility of God. Pushed into marriage by her parents and relatives, she fled to the altar. What better place than where virginity is offered in sacrifice? That was not the end of her courage. Standing before the altar of God, a pure offering, a chaste victim, she even caught the priest's right hand and placed it on her head, demanding of him to say the appropriate prayer. Not tolerating a moment's delay, she bowed her head below the altar and said: "What better veil can I have than the altar which blesses all veils? With this veil Christ, the head of us all, is daily consecrated. My parents and friends, you may stop worrying yourselves about arranging a marriage for me; now my arrangements are over and done with. Perhaps you even have a husband lined up for me. Well, I have found a better one. You may rave about the riches of your choice, boast of his lineage and possessions, but mine is beyond all such comparisons; he has the riches of the universe, he has power over everything, he has heaven for nobility. If you have picked one to equal him, I shall not refuse your choice. If you have not, then you are not providing for my good but only depriving me of it."

66. There was silence. Then suddenly one of them said: "If your father were alive today would he allow you to remain unmarried like this?" Controlling her filial affection with her strong faith she replied: "Perhaps his death was designed by God to remove such hindrance." The objector found that her words about her father could be taken as an oracle about himself, for he died soon after. Then all the others, fearing a like fate for themselves, swung round from opposition to favor, and so the girl's virginity meant no loss of her rightful inheritance; and she had besides the wages of holiness. Girls, you see how devotion is rewarded; and you parents, can see what comes of creating opposition.

THE SECOND BOOK

1. In the first book I have tried to explain, not very successfully, I fear, what a gift virginity is. My idea was that the heavenly charm of the gift would automatically entice the reader.

2. This second book aims at training oneself by learning the main principles to govern one's actions. I must confess to being poor at giving advice and quite unequal to teaching, for the master ought to be above his pupil. That I may not seem to have failed in my undertaking, or to have undertaken too much, I shall try to teach by examples instead of rules. Example is a good teacher; when a thing has been done before it cannot seem impossible now; what has stood the test of time looks sound; what has been transmitted by hereditary practice is worthy of respect.

3. I may be accused of foolhardiness. I should prefer the charge to be rather one of excessive submission; when asked for instruction, I could not very well refuse. I preferred to risk a shameful performance rather than oppose the wish of those whose pursuit wins the sweet favor of God. I cannot be accused of presumption, because though they had their own sources of instruction already and had no need for mine, they asked for words of encouragement. My ready submission can also be excused, for though they had the authority of a martyr, Cyprian, to guide their observance, I thought it useful to have my coaxing words enticing them to that observance. A good teacher can cure defects by dint of severity, but since I am no teacher, I must use persuasion instead.

4. In other places, many have asked for my sermons, so I now write this book to carry my voice to them; as they hold my words in their hands they cannot feel that I have kept away from them. So, I begin.

5. Take as your perfect picture of virginity the life of Mary. It gives you the image of chastity and ideal virtue with all the clarity of a mirror. From it you may read examples of how to live, holy lessons on what to correct, what to avoid, what to hold fast.

Mary's example

6. The first stimulus to learning is the reputation of the teacher, and who is nobler than the mother of God? Who is more splendid than the mother chosen by Splendour itself? Who can be more chaste than she who gave birth without bodily stain? How can I list her virtues? She was virgin not just in body but also in mind; no deceit ever sullied her pure sincerity. She was lowly of heart, wise of speech, prudent of soul, reticent, studious. She placed no hope in the uncertainty of riches but rather in the prayer of poverty. She was attentive to her tasks, modestly making God rather than man the judge of her inner thoughts. She offended no one, was kind to all, respected her seniors, envied none of her companions, shunned ostentation, was guided by reason, loved virtue.

When did even a look of hers ever upset her parents, when did she ever have a disagreement with relatives? She never tired of the lowly, never scoffed at the weak or avoided the poor; and she entered only those meetings of men where charity and modesty had their place. There was nothing forbidding in her looks, nothing arrogant in her words, nothing unbecoming in her actions. Her deportment was never unseemly, her gait never unrestrained, her voice never impatient; the beauty of her body was but an image of her soul, a picture of its goodness. You can tell a good house from its doorway. As soon as you first step into it you know that you will find no ugliness within. When the mind is not darkened by the body's encumbrance, it resembles the inner light which shines out from a lantern.

7. I need say nothing about her fasting or her labors. The latter went beyond the limits of nature, the former hardly allowed for nature's needs. Her good works went on without intermission; her days of fasting were innumerable. When she did have to take food, it was the most ordinary kind, the sort to stave off death rather than provide enjoyment. Sleep came of necessity rather than desire, and even while she slept her spirit was alert, recalling what she had read or continuing what she had been attending to, considering arrangements already made or yet to be made.

8. She never left her home except to go to the temple, and even then, she went with her parents or relatives. Busy within the solitude of her home, she was always guarded by company when she went outside it. But her safest guardian was herself, for her deportment and address commanded respect; every step she took was a step on the road of virtue. A virgin must have others to guard her body, but for her virtues she herself is the guard. She may learn of many teachers, but if virtue is her mistress she can teach: every good action will carry its lesson. Mary was ready to listen to everyone as if everyone could instruct her, but her every act was so full of virtue as to be that of teacher rather than pupil.

9. Thus the evangelist portrays her; thus, the angel found her, and the Spirit chose her. I need not dwell on other points, the love her parents had for her, the praises of others, her worthiness to be the mother of God. When the angel came

to her, she was alone in the inner recesses of her home, for she allowed no one to interrupt the attention of her prayer, or disturb it. She needed no women for companions; her own thoughts were company enough, and she seemed least alone when she was alone. Indeed, how could she be alone living in the company of so many books, so many archangels, so many prophets?

10. There Gabriel, as was his habit, came to her and Mary was disturbed at seeing him in the form of a man, as though he were a stranger; but she recognized him on hearing his name. She felt a stranger to the man, but not to the angel. From this you can see how holy was her hearing, how modest her sight. On being saluted she kept silent but replied when addressed.

Aspects of Mary's virtues

11. Although disturbed at first, she soon promised her obedience. The scripture also shows her charity to her kinsfolk. As soon as she knew that she was chosen by God she became all the humbler and at once went to visit her relative in the mountains. Not that she needed support to make her believe what had happened; she had believed the moment it was announced, and so Elizabeth said (Lk 1:45): "Blessed art thou for thy believing." She remained with Elizabeth three long months, not to confirm her belief but to exercise her charity. She gave this service even after John, his devotion outstripping nature, had leaped for joy in the womb of his mother and greeted Mary as Mother of the Lord.

12. Amid all the other wonders—the barren women bearing child, the virgin conceiving, the dumb man speaking, the Magi adoring, Simeon waiting, the stars giving their message—Mary, though disturbed by the angel's entry, remained unmoved

and "treasured up all these sayings and reflected on them in her heart." (Lk 2:19) Although now the Lord's mother, she still wanted to learn his precepts; though she had conceived God she still desired to know God. (Lk 2:19).

13. She even went every year to Jerusalem at the solemn feast of the Passover, along with Joseph. Allied to each one of her virtues is modesty, which is the essential adjunct of virginity. And so Mary never went to the Temple without Joseph, the guardian of her modesty.

14. Such is the picture of virginity. Such is Mary, whose one life may serve as model for all lives. If the artist pleases us, let us adopt the masterpiece and win its rewards by copying it. What a brilliant variety of virtues sparkles in this one virgin: secluded modesty, manifest faith, devout service.

15. We find her a recluse at home, a companion when serving others, a mother in the temple. She will meet many other virgins and embracing each one will take her to the Lord saying: "This virgin has kept the bridal chamber of my Son free from stain." And Christ himself will commend them to his Father, repeating his prayer: "Father, these are they I have kept for you, on whom the Son of Man has rested his head. I ask that where I am they also may be. And since they did not live just for themselves, let their benefits extend to others; let them be the redemption of parents and brothers. Just Father, the world has not known me, but these have known me and have refused to know the world." (John 17: 23–24).

16. What a triumph will then be seen, what joy of applauding angels at the virgin entering the life of heaven after living a heavenly life on earth! Then Mary will take the tambourine and will lead the virginal dances chanting praise to the Lord for having passed safely through the sea of the world uninjured by its waves. Each will rejoice and say: "I will go up

to the altar of God, the giver of triumphant happiness" (Ps 42:4). "I will offer to God a sacrifice of praise and perform my vows to the Most High" (Ps. 49.14).

17. I am certain that heavenly altars will be ready for you: indeed, I feel that your minds are themselves altars on which Christ every day is immolated for the redemption of the flesh. If the virgin's body is the temple of God surely her soul is like an altar veiled by the hand of the eternal Priest, from which the smoke of divine fire arises out of the embers of the body. Happy are you virgins, redolent of immortal grace, like flowers in a garden, prayer in a temple, a priest at his altar.

The example of St. Thecla

18. Let Mary set your discipline of life. And let Thecla show you how life may be sacrificed. This girl refused marriage and so aroused the anger of her suitor. But she changed even the nature of beasts by the respect her virginity inspired. When thrown to them she freely offered herself to a fierce lion to avoid the gaze of men. This action made those who had turned immodest eyes upon her withdraw them in reverence.

19. The lion lay on the ground and licked her feet, showing by his mute gesture that he could not attack her sacred body. That beast worshipped his prey, and forgetful of his own instincts, seemed to assume the human nature which men had abandoned. By an exchange of natures, men assumed brutality and urged on the animal to cruelty, but the beast, caressing the feet of the virgin, was an object lesson in humanity. Virginity compels even the admiration of lions. Though hungry, the sight of their prey did not move them; their impulse, though aroused, did not master them; though goaded on, their rage did not compel them. They were not held even by habit; their savage nature did not possess them.

They preached piety by their respect. They preached chastity as well by modestly kissing her feet, lowering their eyes to earth as if indicating in awe that neither man nor beast should look upon her naked body.

20. Someone will say: "Why have you brought forward the example of Mary? It is hardly likely that we will manage to be like the Mother of God. And Thecla? Remember that she was trained by the Teacher himself. Give us a master like him if that is the sort of pupil you want." Perhaps then a more modern example will show you that the Apostle is not just the master of one virgin, but of all.

The hidden woman of Antioch

21. Lately in Antioch there lived a dedicated maiden, secluded from the view of men. But the more she gave herself to a hidden life the more she aroused their desire. Hearsay beauty that is not on display is even more desirable, for both love and knowledge acted as incentives: no defect is on view, and beauty is enhanced by not being judged by the eye but chosen in love by the soul. Thecla made a public profession of chastity, that the flame of men's desire might not be fanned by any chance of possessing. This hidden beauty damped their ardor and changed their love into hate. And so came her ordeal.

22. Unable to flee and therefore anticipating an attack on her modesty, she steeled her soul for brave action. Her piety was such that she did not fear death, and her chastity desired it. The day of her battle arrived and everybody was on the *alert.* The girl was brought out ready for the double fight of chastity and of faith. When her enemies saw her constancy in professing her faith, her fear of violation, her readiness to undergo torture, her blushes in front of the spectators, they tried to devise a way of undoing her faith by pretending

to respect her chastity, hoping that by removing the greater they could then undo the lesser. Alternatives were ordered: she could either sacrifice to the gods or else be installed in a brothel. What a religion which devises such penalties!

23. What kind of lives can these people lead if they pronounce judgments like that? She, of course, had no doubts about professing her faith, but she had fears about her modesty, and she said to herself: "What am I to do? It is either martyrdom or virginity. It seems I must lose one of these two crowns. But I can hardly call myself a virgin if I forfeit my belief in the author of virginity. How can I be a virgin if I worship a harlot? And how can I be a virgin if I make love to adulterers, if I solicit desire? It is better to be virgin in the spirit than virgin in the flesh. Perfection means both, but, failing that, I ought to be chaste in God's sight rather than in man's. Although Rahab was a harlot, her belief in God brought her salvation. Judith decked herself out to please an adulterer, but nobody dubbed her an adulteress for she acted through piety and not through passion. She is a good model for me: by entrusting herself to religion she was able to save her chastity and her country. And so if I hold my faith I may save my chastity also. If Judith had decided to keep her modesty at the expense of her religion, well, when her country had gone, her chastity would have gone too."

24. Instructed by such examples she thought also of the Lord's words (Mt 10:39): "It is the man who loses his life for my sake that will secure it." She shed tears, but she did not speak, for she did not want adulterers even to hear her voice. She would not consent to any offence against her chastity, determined to preserve all for Christ. It is hard to see how that body of hers could ever have been violated when even its voice she kept inviolate.

25. Speech fails me as I come to the narration of horrid deeds. Virgins of God, close your ears to the story of this one taken to the house of ill fame. No, open your ears, for though she may be conducted to such a place she still cannot be tarnished, for wherever she is, there too is the temple of God. A brothel cannot defile chastity, but chastity can purify even such a place.

26. Lustful people congregated at the door. It is of no profit to give you a description of the place, but only the wonders accomplished by martyrdom there. There our chaste dove was enclosed, with the vultures ravening outside, vying with each other to be first to catch the prey. But she raised her hands to heaven as if she were in a chapel rather than in this resort of lust. "O Christ," she said, "as you have tamed fierce lions for me, your virgin, now you must tame the brutal minds of men. Cool rain came from the fiery furnace for the three Chaldean youths, and the wave stood still for the Israelites, when your mercy set aside the law of nature. Susanna in the place of punishment bent her knee in prayer and triumphed over adulterers. The hand of him who interfered with the gifts in your temple withered. Now your temple itself is under attack, and as you then prevented theft, now prevent sacrilege. May your name now too be praised if I who have come to the place of sin, go out a virgin."

The Roman soldier appears

27. She had scarcely finished her prayer when in rushed a soldier of terrible appearance. She trembled; indeed, even the crowd trembled, as it gave way to his entry. But the sacred writings came to mind, and she said to herself: "Daniel went to see the punishment of Susanna and though all the people had condemned her he was able to free her. Here too a lamb may

be hiding in wolf's clothing. For Christ has his soldiers: he has his legions. Perhaps of course this man is my executioner; still I need not be afraid, for it is he who makes martyrs." At this we may say to her, "Your faith has saved you." (Lk 8:48).

28. The soldier spoke: 'Sister, please do not be afraid, for I have come as a brother to save your life and not to destroy it. Obey me and you will be safe. I have entered in the guise of lust but if you are willing, I shall go out a martyr. Let us exchange clothing; the same size fits us both—fits Christ too. Your dress will make of me a true soldier and mine will keep you a virgin. My clothing will be to your advantage, and I shall do better without it, for I shall soon be detected. Take it then to hide your womanhood and give me yours to make me a martyr. Put on my cloak to hide your limbs and protect your modesty. My cap will hide your hair and features; on their way out of brothels men usually hide their faces. Once out do not turn your face to look back. Think of the wife of Lot who lost her life because she looked round, even with chaste eyes, at the impure. And do not be afraid that the sacrifice will be deficient. I give myself for you as a victim to God; you give yourself for me as a soldier to Christ, waging the good warfare of chastity and serving for everlasting pay. You have the breastplate of justice (Eph 6:14) to enclose your body spiritually and the shield of faith to withstand attacks; you have also the helmet of salvation, for our salvation is where Christ is, and as man is head of the woman, Christ is head of the virgin."

29. Saying this he took off his cloak. She still had suspicions that he might be an executioner or adulterer. In fact, as he was handing her the cloak, she bent her neck forward to receive his blow. What a spectacle, what a wonder of grace, this contest in a brothel over martyrdom! Between a soldier and a maiden! Though normally very different, the mercy of

God here makes them similar, and the saying is fulfilled (Is 65:25): "Wolf and lamb shall feed together." Not only will they feed together, but they will also be offered together. To get on with the story: through her change of garb the girl escaped from the snare; she flew away, as if carried on invisible wings. This is something the world never saw before, a virgin emerging from a brothel. But she was a virgin of Christ.

30. "Having eyes but seeing not" they all waited outside, like ravenous wolves waiting to devour a lamb. One more shameless than the others entered, but when he noticed the change he said: "What on earth is this? A girl came in here; but this is a man. This is not the old fable where a girl was turned into a hind, but a real case of a virgin becoming a soldier. I once heard, without of course believing the story, that their Christ changed water into wine. Now apparently, he has begun to change the sexes. I must get out of here while I still have the same shape. Maybe I have undergone change already; I am seeing things I didn't expect to see. I came to a brothel and in it I see a woman's substitute and security. I certainly am going out a changed man: I came in an adulterer and I am going out chaste."

31. When the truth was out, the man of course was condemned instead of the virgin in whose place he was found, and so he had his victory and reward. But what really came from that brothel was not one virgin but two martyrs. The story goes on that the girl ran to the scene of his execution and there both began to contend over dying. He said: "I am under sentence of death and that sentence which binds me absolves you." But she said: "I did not want you to replace me at death but only to defend my chastity. As far as chastity is concerned that contract is valid; but as for death I do not want a surety for I can pay my own debt. The sentence really devolves on me; it was pronounced on my behalf. Suppose

you were my bail financially and I did not turn up and the judge ordered your money to be handed over; surely you would have ground for prosecuting me; you could force me to fulfil my contract out of my patrimony, and if I refused, I should be considered worthy of death.

Now this is a case where a much higher debt is at stake. Now is the time for me to die innocent, for I don't want to die guilty later. I have no other choice but this: today I shall be either guilty of another's blood or a martyr in my own. As I have come back here in time how can I be excluded from execution? If I have made any delay, I am all the less innocent. I face a double accusation: my own flight and your death. My body refuses violation, but not death; a virgin may not tolerate profanation, but she may accept the blows of martyrdom. I rejected dishonor, but I am not letting martyrdom go with you. It was my garment that I gave away, not my profession. If you take the chance of death away from me, you have not saved me; you have only deceived me. Please do not contest the prize; do not contradict me. Do not take away the benefit which you have conferred. By denying me this sentence you are imposing the former one upon me, merely exchanging the one for the other. One will cancel out the other and if this last one does not bind me then the other certainly will. Both of us can fulfil our sentences if you allow me to be executed first. In your case death is the only penalty they can make you pay; but for me, my chastity will be again thrown into danger. Surely things will sound better for you if they say you turned a prostitute into a martyr, and not the other way round!'

32. What do you think was the result of their wrangling? Both won! There was no need for a division of the prize. Each conferred the blessing of martyrdom on the other, the one laying its foundation, the other putting on the finishing touches.

Damon and Pythias

33. The philosophic schools laud to the skies the friendship of two Pythagoreans, Damon and Pythias. One of these on being condemned to death asked for time to settle his affairs. The shrewd tyrant who condemned him, fearing he would see him no more, asked him to provide as security someone who would undergo death in his stead if he failed to return on time. I cannot say which of these two philosophers one should prefer. Both excelled. One deserved to find a substitute to face death; the other freely offered himself as such a security. The accused was late in arriving for execution, but his bail prepared for death, looking quite placid, and he was on the point of being killed when his friend returned and offered his neck for the blow. The tyrant wondering at the fact that among these philosophers, friendship was more important than life, asked for admission to their fellowship. Virtue that could convert a tyrant like that was surely powerful.

34. The deed is very praiseworthy, but it is of less account than the former one. These philosophers were two men, but in our story one of the two was a virgin who had to overcome the weakness of her sex. The philosophers were friends but our two were total strangers. There you had only one tyrant, here there were several, and fiercer ones. That one tyrant was able to spare life, these others killed. One philosopher was doomed to die, but here both were free to save themselves. The Pythagoreans had friendship as the end of their endeavor; ours, much wiser, had before their eyes the crown of martyrdom. The former was a human end, the latter divine.

The tyrant cheats his god

35. Since I have mentioned this tyrant, I think I ought to tell you his view of his own gods. You will get an idea of how

useless the gods are when even their worshippers can ridicule them. He went into the temple of Jupiter and ordered the gold garment to be removed from the statue of this god, and a woollen one to be put in its place He remarked that gold was far too light for winter wear, and too heavy for the summer. A joke at the god's expense, as if he was upset by heavy clothes or by the cold! The king noticed too that the god Aesculapius had a golden beard, and this also he had removed, saying that it was quite improper that the son should have a beard while his father Apollo had not yet managed to grow one. He also took some gold cups out of the hands of the statues, saying that after all he was just taking what they were offering him. Men always pray, he said, for good things from the gods and among good things there is nothing better than gold; if you take the view that gold is an evil, well then, the gods ought not to have it in their possession. If, of course, it is a good, men can do with it, being able, unlike the gods, to make some use of it.

36. All through, then, the gods got the worst of the joke, Jupiter not being able to keep his clothes, nor Aesculapius his beard—and Apollo being unable to grow a beard. All these so-called gods were incapable of holding on to their cups, not because they feared the thief, but because they were just dead. Who could worship the like of these, with no power to defend themselves, as we expect of gods, and no power even of hiding, as men have?

37. When Jeroboam the bad king came to the temple of the true God and took the gifts which his father had placed there and began to offer them to idols, on the sacred altar, his right hand withered as he stretched it out. The idols he invoked were of little help to him then. But when he turned to the Lord and asked for pardon, immediately that hand, withered

by sacrilege, was healed by piety. In that one instant you have a meeting of divine anger and divine mercy. His hand was taken from him in his sacrilege, but it was restored to him in his penitence.

Not rules, but examples

38. Holy ones, these words are the little gift I have prepared for you—rather crudely, I fear, for I have been bishop for less than three years. But what I have lacked in experience has been taught to me by your practice. I could glean very little experience from my own short apprenticeship in the life of religion. Take whatever flowers you may find in these words as gathered from your own lives. These are not rules given, but examples taken. My words have but painted a picture of your own virtue and in them, as in a mirror, you may see the reflection of your own wisdom. If you have breathed any grace into my mind what comes from it in this writing is yours. Personal tastes differ, and if my book contains anything clear and simple it is for all of you; but if there is something of stronger taste, that can be tried by the more perfect. If you find anything of modesty, let it stay in your hearts and affect your actions. If there is anything flowery here, the flower of your lives need not refuse it.

39. For I have tried to inspire love in the spouse, as it is written (Deut 6:5): "Thou shalt love the Lord thy God." For the marriage feast I have tried to tie a garland round the head of my discourse: "Clap hands and stamp feet." (Ezek 6:11). I have tried to scatter roses on the couch of these eternal nuptials. Even in temporal nuptials the bride hears compliments before she comes to obeying orders. Hard duties need not trouble her, before her love is strengthened by the nourishment of tenderness.

Love enables free self-gift

40. Horses, even though wild and swift, love the sound of their neck being patted and coaxed into accepting the yoke. They hear the soft word before they feel the whip. But when their necks have taken the yoke, they are held with the rein and urged on with the spur and must work in pairs and obey the horseman. Similarly, she ought first to have her enjoyment of the divine love, to admire from the doorway the golden posts of her heavenly bridal couch, to see the doorway decorated with garlands; and to listen from within to the choral song outside. So, she will not withdraw in fear from the yoke of the Lord but will submit to it freely when called.

41. Venture forth from Lebanon, and come to me, my bride, my queen that shall be." (Song 4:8) In the chant we meet that verse over and over, and so the virgin can follow these words of the Lord if she does not trust those of men. That teaching is not my invention; it is what I have received. It is what we find in the heavenly poem (Song 1:1): "A kiss from those lips! Wine cannot ravish the senses like that embrace, nor the fragrance of rare perfumes match it for delight. Thy very name spoken soothes the heart like flow of oil." All that passage speaks of playful delight, evokes joy, excites love. (Song 1:3): "What wonder the maids should love thee? Draw me after thee where thou wilt; see, we hasten after thee, by the very fragrance of those perfumes allured! To his own bower the king has brought me."

42. Those verses begin with the kiss and end with the bower. But when the virgin grows inured to hard toil and the practice of virtue she can open the gates with her own hand, go into the field, or remain in the fortress. In the beginning, however, she simply ran after the fragrance of perfume. Soon the perfumes are exchanged for the fortress. At the end what

do we read? (Song 8.9): "Steadfast as a wall if she be, that wall shall be crowned with silver." She who formerly played with kisses now builds towers. Turreted with the precious pinnacles of sanctity, she can now both repel hostile attack and build the fortifications of merit.

THE THIRD BOOK

1. In the previous two books I have concluded all I had to say. Now, my dear sister, it is time for me to recall the instructions given by Bishop Liberius of blessed memory; you have often talked to me about them. The great sanctity of this man will lend charm to my words. You recall how on the feast of the Nativity, in Saint Peter's, you made your profession and signified it by your new attire. It was indeed a suitable occasion, the day on which the Virgin received her offspring. Standing roundabout were many holy maidens, all eager to have your company. The bishop said: "My daughter, it is a good marriage you have desired. See what a great crowd has assembled on this birthday of your Spouse. Not one will go away unfed, for your Spouse is he who when called to the wedding changed water into wine. He grants you now the pure sacrament of virginity; up to now you have been subject to the weak elements of bodily matter. Your Spouse is he who with five loaves and two fishes fed four thousand people in the desert and if there had been even more people, he could have fed them. He has called many here to your wedding and it is not now barley loaves which he gives but his own body from heaven.

2. Today as man he was born of the Virgin, though begotten of the Father before all things. In body he resembles his mother, but in power he is equal to the Father. Only begotten on earth and in heaven, God of God, offspring of the Virgin, Justice of the Father, Omnipotent from Omnipotent, Light from Light, equal to the Father, not different from him in power, not confused with him through any expression or

extension of term that would make them one, but distinct from him in virtue of generation. Your spouse is divine: without him the things of heaven and sea and earth could not exist. He is the good Word of the Father which "was in the beginning." (Jn 1:1). That phrase shows his eternity, and the words "was with the Father" show his power undivided and inseparable from that of the Father. "And the Word was God": a sign of his divinity.

3. On this brief statement of truth you may base your faith. Love him, daughter, for he is good (Mk 10:18): "None is good but God alone." If it is certain that the Son is God and that God is good, then it is clear that the Son is the good God. Love him, I repeat. He was begotten eternally by the Father before the dawn-star, begotten as Son, uttered from the heart as the Word. In him the Father was well pleased. He is the strong arm of the Father because he is the Creator of all; he is the Wisdom of the Father because he proceeds from the mouth of God; he is the power of the Father, because in him resides corporally the fulness of the divinity. The Father so loved him as to carry him in his bosom and place him on his right hand in wisdom and power.

4. As Christ is the power of God the question may be raised: was there a time when God was without power, a time when the Father was without the Son? No: the Father always was, and the Son always was. As the Father is perfect, so the Son is perfect. What detracts from the power of the Son detracts from him whose power it is. In perfect divinity there is no inequality. Love him then whom the Father loved; honor him whom the Father honored: "To deny reverence to the Son is to deny reverence to the Father who has sent him. To deny the Son is to deny the Father." (Jn 5:23). So much for your faith.

5. "But sometimes when faith is safe enough youth is the weak point. Take therefore a little wine to keep up the strength of your body, but do not take it for pleasure, for youth and wine are alike incentives to vice. Let fasting too restrain your youth; let meager food hold, as with a chain, all inordinate desires; let reason check them, let hope tame them, let fear hold them. The person who cannot restrain desires is, as it were, dragged by wild horses, tossed and bruised and torn and trampled.

Diana and Hippolytus

6. There is a story that this once happened to the young man, Hippolytus, because of Diana's love. The story is ornamented with poetic details. Neptune, piqued because his rival has been preferred to him, struck madness into the horses of Hippolytus, and, displaying his power, overcame the youth not by bravery but by deceit. That is why at the yearly sacrifice to Diana a horse is offered on her altars. This lady, though they call her a virgin, was in love with someone who had no love for her, a fault that even whores avoid. There I leave the story. I think it less shameful that a young man should be inflamed with love for a wanton woman and lose his life through it than those two gods, as they are called, should fight over the crime. They say that Jupiter was angered by his sinful daughter's grief and took vengeance on Asclepius, the physician who restored Hippolytus to life so that he could sin with Diana in the woods. Certainly, Diana was a good huntress of wild beasts, but she hunted desires as well, and wild ones at that.

7. They may grant Neptune his power and fury if they add in his sinful love. They may allow Diana command of her woods if they stress the sin she performed there. They may attribute to Asclepius the raising of the dead, so long as they

admit that he himself when struck by Jupiter's thunderbolt was unable to escape. They may let Jupiter have his fictitious thunderbolts if they also proclaim his shameful deeds.

Prudence and Modesty

8. "From these myths let us return to our purpose. I advise frugality in all foods which stimulate the body. Flesh attracts even the eagles down to earth, and to your heart belongs the inner eagle of which we read, "He restores thy youth, as the eagle's plumage is restored." (Ps 103:5). Your lofty and swift virginal flight must know none of the appetites of the flesh. Avoid banquets, flee from perilous conversations.

9. For the younger I think that visits, if they must be made to parents or companions, should be few. In these acts of dutifulness, modesty wears away, boldness of manner appears and levity creeps in. Modesty goes while you are trying to be courteous. If you fail to reply to a question, you seem impolite; if you do reply you are caught in idle gossip. I should prefer you to be deficient in conversation rather than overdo it. In church, women are not allowed to speak even about divine things; they must wait and ask their questions at home. That rule must be even stricter for one in whom modesty is the adornment of her age and silence its keeper.

10. Is Rebecca not a good example of such modesty? When she first saw her spouse, she put on her veil so that she should not be looked upon until she was wed. She was not afraid of looking less beautiful but only of being less modest. And Rachel: did she not grieve when Jacob kissed her? She would have gone on weeping had she not recognized him as her cousin. So, she retained both her modesty and her affection. To men the command is issued, "Nor let thy eyes linger on a maid unwed, whose very beauty may take thee unawares." (Sir

9:5). What must be said then to a consecrated virgin, who by loving sins in her heart and by being loved sins in very deed?

11. There is great virtue in silence, especially in the church. No phrase of the holy readings will escape you if you have an attentive ear and restrain your tongue. No word you might later wish unsaid will pass your lips if you mistrust your speech. There is much sin in much speaking. It was said to the homicide (Gen 4:7): "You have sinned; be silent," that he might sin no more. To the virgin we must say: "Be silent that you may not begin to sin." We read that Mary kept in her heart all the things that were said about her Son. You also, when you hear from the reading that Christ is about to come, or that he has come, do not cause disturbance by talking, but attend to the fact. Is there anything more undignified than raising obstruction to the divine oracles, preventing them from being heard, from being believed, from being revealed, surrounding the sacrament with a babble of voices, impeding the prayer pronounced for the salvation of all?

The virtue of silence

12. The pagans show the reverence of silence to their idols. Valerius Maximus tells the story that when Alexander the Great, king of Macedon, was once offering sacrifice, a barbarian boy who was attending to the lights got his sleeve on fire and although he suffered severe burns, he remained motionless and did not show his pain by groaning or even by quiet weeping. His reverence was such as to overcome nature. And remember that he need not have feared the gods, for they didn't exist, but only the king; those gods would have burned like himself if the fire had caught them.

13. My point is put better by the playwright Terence. In one of his plays a certain father is giving a banquet, and he warns

his son not to talk unbecomingly about his shady love affairs, giving him this command—which you, virgin of God, when you attend the liturgy might well take to heart: "No groans, no calls, no coughing, no laughing, please." What he was able to do at a banquet can you not manage at the divine mysteries? Virginity should show itself first in the voice. Modesty should seal your lips, religion dispel their weakness, habit train them. Seriousness of manner should declare the virgin to me with her obvious modesty, her sober gait, her reserved countenance. Clear signs of virtue must attend her as heralds of her virginity. She is not much of a virgin if you cannot recognize her as such when you see her.

14. The story is often told that on one occasion the noise of croaking frogs distracted a congregation of the faithful from attending to their prayer. The priest ordered the frogs to be silent and to reverence the sacred mysteries. Suddenly all around they ceased their noise. If the living things of the swamp keep silence, can men not do so? If the animal without reason reverently recognized what nature could not tell him, is man going to be so irreverent as not to give the same attention to his religious rites as he gives to any pleasant sound he hears?

15. Those were the words Bishop Liberius of holy memory spoke to you. Others might have found his precepts too lofty; but you by your observance have made them seem small. Your virtue has equaled his teaching, and even surpassed it. Fasting is one of his rules, but only at special times. But you multiply these nights and days and pass long periods without food. Sometimes when you are requested to take some, to put away your book for a little while, your immediate reply is (Mt 4:4): "Man cannot live by bread only: there is life for him in all the words which proceed from the mouth of God." Your banquet always consists of the coarsest food, almost the sort

to make you eager for more fasting. Your drink is just water from the stream. Penance goes with your prayer; sleep overtakes you still holding your book.

Training for maturity

16. All this is fitting for the years of youth, until the spirit is trained into maturity. But once a virgin has raised her trophy over the conquered body, she ought to relax the rigor somewhat that she may live on as the teacher of a younger age. An old vine overloaded with shoots easily gives way unless it gets an occasional pruning. In its youth, of course, it may be let to grow abundantly, but in age it ought to be pruned so that it does not put out a lot of empty wood or die through overproduction. The good husbandman protects his vine by tending the soil and shelters it from frost and from the burning mid-day sun. He also tills his farm in rotation. If he cannot let it lie idle, he at least changes what he sows, so that the fields may find rest in the change of crops. You too, virgin of years, sow the hillocks of your soul with different seeds; temperate eating at one time, temperate fasting at another, reading, work, prayer. So, the variety of your life will be a guarantee of repose.

17. A whole farm cannot be given over to one crop. Here rising along the hills, you have the vines; there you have the ripening olives, there fragrant roses. Often the sturdy farmer, as a change from the plough, works the soil with his hands as he puts down his plants, and the same strong hands that guide the toiling oxen through the rows of vines will gently milk the sheep. The more varied the crop, the better the field. Take this example from the good farmer; do not keep the plough of your fasting in the soil all the time. Let there grow in your garden the rose of modesty, the lily of thought, and

have your flowerbeds watered by the divine Blood. You know the proverb about all work and no play. Of course, there has to be special penance on the days of Lent, though nothing must ever be for the sake of show, but only for love of God.

Frequent prayer

18. Frequent prayer must commend us to God. David said, "Votive thanks I give thee seven times a day." (Ps 118:164). He was able to do that although occupied with the duties of his kingdom. It is even more necessary for us to do it, for we read, "Watch and pray that you do not enter into temptation." (Mt 26:41). Certainly, we must offer solemn prayers and thanksgiving at set times: when we rise from sleep, when we go out, before taking food, after taking it, at the evening hour of incense, and as we are going to bed.

19. Even when in bed it is good to repeat the Psalms, alternating them with the Lord's own prayer. You can do this whenever you wake up or in the interval before sleep overcomes you. Thus, the beginning of your rest will be freed from worldly cares and sleep will catch you thinking of divine things.

Pythagoras, the inventor of the term "philosophy," used to get a flute-player every evening to play soft music for him before he went to bed, to soothe away the cares of the day. This was of course, as they say, a fool's game, trying to banish temporal cares using temporal things. He contaminated himself even more by seeking purification in pleasure. We must be clear of all earthly vices and free our minds from the contagion of the flesh.

20. We should meditate upon the Creed every morning; it is the seal we have on our heart. We should also recite it when we feel afraid of anything. You never find a soldier in tent or on the battlefield without his military emblem.

Present weeping, future joy

21. Surely the saying of the prophet makes for our instruction (Ps 6:6): "Every night I lie weeping on my bed, until the tears drench my pillow." If we take this literally it means a great flood of the tears of prayer drenching the bed. Present weeping betokens joy in the future (Lk 6:21): "Blessed are you who weep now; you will laugh for joy." If we take the word "bed" to refer to the body, then it means that we should wash away the sins of the body with the tears of penance. We read (Song 3:9): "A litter King Solomon will have of Lebanon wood; a golden frame it must have, on silver props, with cushions of purple, and it is studded inside with gems." What is that litter but a picture of our body? The bright gems signify air, the gold fire, the silver water, the wood earth; and of these four elements the human body is made. In the bed of that body our soul reclines unless it is out upon the rough places of the hills, restless on the hard earth. Raised above vices by that wood the soul reposes. David says (Ps 41:3): "The Lord will sustain him when he lies on his bed of pain." You can talk of a "bed of pain" only if it has the power of feeling. The body that suffers pain is the body doomed to death (Rom 7:24): "Pitiable creature that I am, who is to set me free from a nature thus doomed to death?"

22. As we have alluded to the Lord's body, no reader need be disturbed that the Lord took on a body of pain; he ought to recall that the Lord grieved and wept at the death of Lazarus, that his body was wounded in the Passion, that from the wound came blood and water, and that he yielded up his spirit. The water was for our cleansing, the blood for our nourishment, the spirit for our resurrection. Christ is at once for us hope, faith and charity; hope in the Resurrection, faith in the washing, love in the sacrament of blood.

23. As he took a body of pain, he allowed it to be racked in infirmity for the benefit of all human flesh. By his Passion our weakness was cured, by his Resurrection death was conquered. Still, we must be sorrowful for the world as well as joyful in the Lord, sorrowful in penance, joyful in gratitude. The Teacher of the nations in a wholesome precept tells us (Rom 12:15): "Rejoice with those who rejoice, mourn with the mourner."

24. In fact if we want to go to the heart of this matter we may turn to the same apostle where he says (Col 3:17): "Whatever you are about, in word and action alike, invoke always the name of the Lord Jesus Christ, offering your thanks to God the Father through him." Every word and every act we must refer to Christ who brought life out of death and light out of darkness. A sick body is sometimes eased by warmth, sometimes by cold; change of temperature, if according to medical advice, is good; but if it is against such advice then it aggravates the disease. What Christ our doctor prescribes is our remedy; what is against his orders is our ruin.

25. Our joy then can only be that of a good conscience; it will not depend on intemperate feastings or amorous melodies. These endanger modesty; their attraction is risky, especially if dancing is added to the entertainment; I want the virgins of God to keep away from that sort of celebration. That expert man of the world, Cicero, said: "Nobody, only a fool, will dance while sober." We gather then from his worldly wisdom that dancing must start with either drunkenness or madness. A stronger warning is that place in the scripture where John, the herald of Christ, was executed by the whim of a dancer; the lure of her dance was more deadly than even the sacrilegious fury of Herod.

Danger of immodesty

26. I must make more than a passing reference to the Baptist. I must note his character, his murderer, the pretext, manner, and occasion of his death. He was killed by the adulterers he had accused; they turned the sentence against their judge. His death was a present to a dancing girl. He was executed during a banquet–a deed that even barbarians would not tolerate. The cruel order for his death was issued; the execution of that savage sentence ran back and forth between banquet-hall and prison. What a collection of sins in a single deed!

27. These fatal banquets were prepared with regal luxury, and now when the crowd was greatest, the daughter of the queen, instructed privately beforehand, came out to dance in the men's sight, with an immodesty she could have learned only from her adulterous mother. Is anything more likely to inflame desires than displaying improper motions of the limbs, which nature or convention prefers to be hidden, wanton play of the eyes, twisting the head and tossing the hair?

28. From this it is an easy step to offence against God. What modesty can possibly result from all this dancing and clapping and disturbance? The king in delight told the girl that she could ask anything she wanted, swearing that if she asked for half his kingdom, he would give it. Notice the light judgment passed by these worldly people on their own worldly powers; they are ready to give away kingdoms in return for a dance. Advised by her mother, the girl asked to have brought to her on a dish the head of John. The king, we are told, was full of remorse. This was not penance, but an admission of his sin, for it is always the divine order that when people do sinful things, they condemn themselves out of their own mouths. "Out of respect to those who sat at table," it says (Mk 6:26). What respect for guests could there be in ordering

a murder? "Out of respect to his oath." What a religion! Perjury would have been better. The Lord in the Gospel wisely tells us not to swear in case there should be risk of perjury and sin. Herod to preserve his oath strikes down the innocent. Though it is hard to say which is the more dreadful, the perjuries of tyrants seem preferable to their oaths.

29. Anyone seeing the rush from the banquet to the prison must surely have thought that the prophet was being liberated. Anyone who heard that the banquet was given to celebrate Herod's birthday and that the girl was given choice of what she wished must have concluded that she had sent word to free John. Why indeed permit cruelty in a banquet, why mix laments with your pleasure? During the banquet, by a command from the table, the prophet was led out to his doom. He did not of course try to avoid execution. He was killed by the sword and his head was brought in on a dish. Cruelty hungered for this dish; brutality, unsatisfied by banqueting, had to feed upon it.

30. Here, cruel king, is a sight to grace your banquet. That nothing may be lacking to your cruelty put out your hand and let this sacred blood run on your fingers. And since your hunger cannot be satisfied by this banquet nor your cruel thirst assuaged by the wine-cup, drink the blood flowing from the veins of this severed head. These eyes even in death are testimony to your crime; they are turned away from the sight of your feasting. These eyes are closed not by death but by horror at your luxury. That golden mouth, now dead, whose sentence you could not bear to hear, is now silent, but you still fear it. That tongue even in the convulsion of death still fulfils its living duty of condemning your incest. John's head is brought to Herodias. She is glad, imagining she has evaded crime by killing the judge.

31. What do you say to all this, holy women? You see what to teach your daughters and what to forbid them. This girl could dance, but she was the daughter of an adulteress. A modest and chaste mother will teach her children piety instead of dancing. You, serious and wise fathers, learn to avoid the banquets of the impious. Such banquets are on a par with their treacherous judgments.

32. My holy sister, Marcellina, my little writing is now at last sailing into harbor. You have been reflecting that the Holy Scripture forbids suicide to Christians and so you have put to me a timely question: How goes it with those who throw themselves from cliffs or into rivers to escape from their persecutors? In the case of virgins faced with the task of defending their virtue I can give a clear answer from the example of the martyrs.

33. Fifteen-year-old Saint Pelagia lived near Antioch with her sisters; they were all virgins. At the outbreak of persecution, she was in her home, her mother and sisters being away, and she found herself surrounded by pirates of faith and chastity. Deprived of all help she still trusted in God. "What will become of my virginity?" she asked. "Unless I am careful it will be taken from me. I desire my own death, but I fear it at the same time. I fear it because death ought to be received from another and not inflicted by one's own hand. I would readily die if only they would bring it about; but if they don't, I still must die somehow. God will not, I feel sure, be offended by this way of escape, and if perhaps there is some offence faith will clear it away. When I think it over, that cannot be violence if it is voluntary. A worse violence would be to desire to die and find it impossible. Not that I shall find it impossible; who could desire death and miss it when there are so many steep paths leading to it? I will throw myself down from the roof upon the sacrilegious altars, overturn them, and extinguish

their fire with my own blood. My right hand will not have to deal the fatal blow, my heart will not have to recoil from pain. I will leave room for no weakness of my flesh. It does not matter that there is no sword; I can die by my own method, without any aid from an executioner, in the bosom of my motherland."

Domnina and her daughters flee

34. She adorned her head and put on a bridal robe as if going to her wedding rather than her death. When she was dead and the persecutors saw that their virginal prize had been snatched away from them, they began to hunt instead for her mother, Domnina, and her sisters, Bernice and Prodose. These, their flight supported by the spirit, were already escaping over the fields of chastity. But their persecutors closed upon them from behind and in front they found a river barring their flight and hemming them in for martyrdom. "What have we to fear?" they said. "Look, here is water; what is to hinder us from being baptized? (Acts 8:36). In this baptism we can lose our sins and gain a kingdom, and then there can be no further sin. Let us then enter water which has the power of regenerating, the baptism which makes virgins, which opens heaven, covers the weak, hides death, produces martyrs. O God, Creator of all things, we pray that when our spirits have departed the flood may not tear our bodies apart, that death may not separate them in burial since life never separated them in affection. Let there be one bravery for us, one death, one burial."

35. Then girding up their garments modestly to allow them free movement they joined their hands as if dancing and entered the water where the current ran strong and the slope was steep. None of them hesitated or looked for safe foothold, and anxiety arose only on encountering firm footing or shallower water; for they grew happier as the water became

deeper. The mother held her daughters' hands, rejoicing that they were together with her, her only fear being that the waves might separate them. "To you, Christ," she said, "I offer these victims, these examples of chastity, leaders of my journey, companions of my suffering."

36. This constancy of theirs when alive need cause no wonder, for even after death their bodies remained united. The river did not unclothe them or toss them apart in its swift current. To her last breath the mother held her embrace of affection and piety and did not relax it in death. She had done all that piety asked, and affection followed her beyond death. The companions she took with her to martyrdom she kept with her to the tomb.

37. My sister, I need never mention such far-off examples to you, for purity has been infused into you by a sort of heredity from your mother, who was a martyr. It must have been so, for you lived in the country without a director and without sisters for company. No master, no pupil: as you have had no teacher, your virtue must have come by heredity.

38. Your holy mother, Soteris, has been the parent of your soul as well as of your body. In Diocletian's persecution (A.D. 303 to 311) she was treated to all kinds of violent insult before the climax of her agony. Even then she presented her face to the executioner to be struck. Her face had been spared the torture endured by the rest of her body and had been a sort of idle spectator of the other limbs. She offered her tender cheeks to the blows, and so mighty was her patience and endurance that the executioner seemed to grow tired of striking before the martyr tired of punishment. She did not bend her head, did not turn her face away, did not emit sigh or tear. Finally, when all the varieties of punishment had been tried, a sword delivered the deathblow she so eagerly awaited.

DE VIRGINITATE

DE VIRGINITATE

1. Of great renown in antiquity was the judgment given by Solomon when the two women appealed to him in court (1 Kings 3:16). One, you may remember, had killed her infant by lying upon it in her sleep; then she laid false claim to the other's child. The other in love and innocence claimed her own child. Each of them argued her case and Solomon was faced with a difficult decision; he could not discern the inner workings of the minds of the women. In this predicament he called for a sword and asking his servants to pretend to carry out his command, he ordered the child to be cut in two parts, one for each woman. The one agreed readily and even clamored for the division, quite unaffected by motherly love. The real mother, however, was more afraid of losing the child than of losing the case; thinking not of her own comfort but only of the safety of her little charge she asked for it to be given over alive to the other rather than be handed back mutilated to herself. In this way, Solomon, not of course by any divine power but only by exploring the psychology of motherhood, declared that the infant ought to be given back to the woman whose distress over his suggestion showed her to be the true mother. As for the other woman, who showed no pity at the thought of the child's death, he said it was quite unnatural of her to have been so unfeeling.

2. So the truth came out, though it was slowed up by the deceit of the bad mother. Even the good mother had a period of anxious doubt as the judgment hung in the balance. The whole thing happened long ago as a symbol, but

it was written down for our betterment (1 Cor 10:11). It teaches us that all deceits can be brought to light and hidden stratagems revealed.

Faith and temptation

3. My present task is not to discuss these women but what they represent. The two stand for faith and temptation. Temptation has ever been the parent of sin. On losing its offspring by the vice of carnal conversation and mental sloth it tries to abduct the offspring of faith. So, while temptation argues its case in court poor faith hangs in the balance until the sword of Christ sorts out the real affections. Sword of Christ, did I say? Yes: the one of which it is written: "I have come to bring a sword on the earth" (Mt 10:34); the one which is mentioned in the words: "As for thy own soul, it shall have a sword to pierce it" (Lk 2:35). This weapon, this sword, is further described by Paul: "God's word to us is something alive, full of energy; it can penetrate deeper than any two-edged sword, reaching the very division between soul and spirit, between joints and marrow" (Heb 4:12). The sword of God is a good sword, for only a good sword can be a searcher of heart and loins, able to divide falsehood from truth and to preserve, rather than kill, those whose soul it transfixes.

4. So much for the Book of Kings. We have followed the case in the court, the story as told in history, its application to conscience, its relevance to faith. Now let us turn to the passage which we have just heard read from the Book of Judges (Jgs 11:1), a story of parricide which was surely not meant to fall on idle ears. I shall repeat it.

5. Jephte was a Judge of the Israelites. Caught in a dangerous war and fearing the uncertain outcome of battle he made a vow to the effect that if he beat his enemies he would go

home, and the first thing to meet him inside his door he would sacrifice to God, his guide to victory. He did battle, routed his enemies, and came home. At the door his daughter, thinking of his love and knowing nothing of his vow, met him. At once he thought of his promise and the thought filled him with pain. "Alas, daughter," he said, "thou hast undone me; the vow that has once left my lips I must needs fulfil." She answered, "Why father, if thou hast uttered a vow to the Lord, carry out thy promise." But she asked for two months of respite to go out into the hills and bewail the fact that she would die unwed. When the two months were over, she wandered back to her father, and he fulfilled his promise." These latter words are used in euphemism, for Scripture avoids describing the actual deed of parricide.

6. What am to say of all this? Do I approve of the man's action? Certainly not. But though I disapprove of the killing I want to draw attention to his fear and dread of breaking his promise. Note the words spoken to Abraham: "I know now that thou fearest God; for my sake thou was ready to give up thy only son" (Gen 22:12). You have there your proof that a promise is not to be broken lightly. You have also in that same passage proof that parricide is not pleasing to God, for a sheep is put in place of Isaac and receives the deathblow instead of him.

The power of obedience

7. Jephte had Abraham's example to show him that God is not pleased with human blood. The divine message given to Abraham showed that the safety of one's son should be second in importance to religious obedience; children should be offered to God, though not slaughtered to him. As Jephte's daughter was so anxious about her father's vow, why did he

not doubt the wisdom of killing her? Since she tried to obviate infidelity on his part, why did he not try to avoid putting her to death?

8. Someone will ask: why did God prevent the parricide in the one case and in the other let it be carried out? Is he a respecter of persons? No—only of merits and virtues. When the course of action to be taken was doubtful, the divine message had to indicate what was right, both for that occasion and for the future. But once the first event had occurred there was no need for a special intervention in the second; the precedent was sufficient pattern for correct action.

9. Perhaps because their merits were not parallel, one norm would not cover both. In the first case the father grieved, and the daughter cried, both doubting the mercy of God. But Abraham showed no grief and gave no heed to parental feelings; as soon as he heard the divine command, he did not postpone his sacrifice but hastened to obey. Little Isaac had no doubts either as he trotted along behind his father; he shed no tears when he was tied and asked for no delay of the sacrifice. Theirs was the greater faith and it found the readier mercy. There were no tears from the boy whose name means "mother's laughter" (Gen 21:6). In return for his joyful devotion a sheep was ordered to be sacrificed in his stead. He did not seek to evade the immolation of himself, having no doubts about the mercy of God, no worries about his self-immolation. No one was found to restrain his father's worship even though it involved bloodshed, because everyone recognized the duty of offering the whole gift as promised.

10. That bloody sacrifice was offered and there was no opposition. Now in our day is there to be opposition when chastity is the offering? Jephte promised parricide and fulfilled his promise; if a father nowadays vows the offering of his

daughter's integrity is there to be opposition to the sentiment inspiring so good an offering? Jephte's daughter sorrowfully gave her life to save her father's promise; here with us can a holy promise not be fulfilled either through duty to parent or independently?

11. In this matter I myself have come in for criticism. And why? Is it because I have stood in the way of illicit wedlock? Well, on that score they may also blame John the Baptist. Though this perhaps is the only thing in me worthy of praise, they may condemn it as they please, for I have John the prophet on my side. Is he the wrong example to quote? Tell me, what was the cause of his martyrdom? Precisely these words of his: "It is wrong for thee to take her" (Mt 14:4). If this was said about a man's wife how much more aptly may it be said of a virgin consecrated to God? If it was said to a king, how much more easily may it be said to the ordinary citizen? Thank God, there is no Herod here; I can only hope there is no Herodias!

12. Was it wrong of me to speak in defence of virginity? If so, why was it written: "Protect the orphan, give the widow redress"? (Is 1:17). Or why this: "He is a father to the orphan and gives the widow redress?" (Ps 68:5). Shall I desert those dedicated to chaste integrity and turn to condemning them?

How pagans honored virginity

13. At the altar of the Vestal fire the pagans hold virginity in honor. The Vestal virgins have neither holiness nor purity of mind, but they are praised for virginity of the flesh. Nobody excludes these virgins from the pagan rites. Is virginity then to be shut out from the church of God? The pagan girls are forced into virginity though it is not part of pagan dogma; with us is there going to be prevention of what is a matter of

essential doctrine? The pagan girls are enticed by rewards to abstain from marriage; are ours to be forced into marriage by threats? The pagans must use force to recruit their virgins; are we going to use force to prevent their freely dedicating themselves? Can a priest like me stand by without offering his life, if necessary to defend the consecrated virgin's sacrifice?

14. Notice that virgins merited to witness the resurrection of the Lord, even before the Apostles. That is evident from the reading you have heard today. When, according to John, the body of the Lord was laid "in a new tomb," (Jn 19:41), or as Matthew described it, when Joseph had placed the body "in a new grave which he had fashioned for himself" (Mt 27:60), virgins watched over it. Quite rightly do both writers record the detail that it was a new tomb: that rules out the possibility of somebody else rising from an old one.

It is also fitting, in a spiritual sense, that the body was placed in the tomb of a just man (Lk 23:50), for Christ's rising from the dead is in renewal of justice. It was right too, in the letter as in the spirit, that the tomb belonged to another: the Lord did not want any tomb of his own. Burial places do very well for those who are under the law of death, but the conqueror of death has no need for a tomb. Triumphant over death, he had no desire for a grave. The Virgin Mary saw the resurrection of the Lord. She was the first to see and believe. Although Mary Magdalen also saw, she doubted.

Mary Magdalen forbidden to touch Jesus

15. Here, I ask you to notice an important point, which may dispel any doubts you might feel about the Resurrection. Note that the merit of virginity does not depend merely on integrity of the flesh; it needs integrity of mind as well. Mary Magdalen was forbidden to touch the risen Lord (Jn 20:17)

simply because her faith in his rising wavered. Only a firm faith may touch Christ.

16. "But Mary Magdalen stood without before the tomb weeping" (Jn 20:11). The outsider weeps, not the one who is within. She weeps because she does not see the body of Christ, and not seeing it she thinks it has been taken away. Mary stays outside, but not Peter and John. They ran right on and entered. Having then no need to weep they came out in joy. It was because Mary did not enter that she shed tears, and doubted, and got the idea that the body had been stolen. Not even the sight of angels made her believe. The angels said to her: "Woman why art thou weeping? For whom art thou searching"? (Jn 20:13). So the angels spoke, and the Lord himself later repeated it word for word, which goes to show that what angels say is really the command of God.

17. As I say, the Lord repeated the angels' words: "Woman, why art thou weeping? For whom art thou searching?" This non-believer is called "woman"; the believer, on the other hand, rises into "perfect manhood, that maturity which is proportioned to the completed growth of Christ" (Eph 4:13). This word "woman" is not meant as a slight on her sex but only on her hesitation; "virgin" is the name for her who had believed. "Why art thou weeping?": as much as to say: you are the cause of your own trouble, the source of your own tears, for you disbelieve Christ. You weep because you do not see him; if you only believe, you will see him. He is never absent from those who seek him. "Why art thou weeping?" As if to say: this is not an occasion for tears but for a ready faith, a faith worthy of God! If you stop thinking of mortal affairs you will have no tears, for without the thought of things that perish you cannot possibly have reason to weep. Why lament when others are so glad?

18. "Whom do you seek?" Do you not see that Christ is here? Do you not see that Christ is the wisdom of God, that he is holiness, chastity, integrity; that he is born of a Virgin; that he is ever from the Father, with the Father, in the Father; born, not made; not inferior; ever loved; true God from true God.

19. "They have carried away my Lord, she said, and I cannot tell where they have taken him" (Jn 20:13). You are making a mistake, lady, in supposing that Christ was taken from the tomb by others and not risen by his own power. Nobody can take away the power of God, the wisdom of God, divine chastity. Christ cannot be taken from the sepulcher of the just, any more than he can be taken away from the heart of his virgin, from the recesses of holiness. Whoever plans that theft will fail.

20. Then the Lord said to her: "Mary, look upon me." As unbeliever she had been called "woman," but once her conversion begins she gets the same name as the mother of Christ, for now she is a soul which gives birth to Christ spiritually. "Look upon me." The person who looks on Christ is set on the right path, but the one who does not goes astray.

21. So she turned and looked at him and said "Rabbi," which means Master. A look like that means conversion, and conversion in turn makes vision still keener, for the very sight means improvement. So now she hails as "Master" the Christ she had thought dead, talks to the one she had imagined stolen.

22. "Do not cling to me thus," he said (John 20.17). Even though she now makes some attempt at correction still her disposition of doubt is not allowed to touch Christ. "Do not cling to me thus": do not touch the power of God, the wisdom of God, holy purity, divine chastity.

23. "But return to my brethren." Leave off your weeping outside the tomb and go to his devoted priests, his picked men, and "tell them this: I am going up to him who is my Father and your Father, who is my God and your God" (Jn 20:17). In other words: Woman, do not raise questions here. Ask those who are more perfect, and they will tell you about the distinction between "my Father" and "your Father." My Father by divine generation is your father by adoption. By "my Father" the Son of God distinguished himself from creatures, and by "your Father" he indicates our grace of spiritual adoption. The words "my God" refer to the mystery of his Incarnation. Although he is Son of the Father by nature, he says "my God" with reference to the sacrament of the body he has assumed. "Your God" on the other hand denotes the action of his redemption within us.

24. God has truly become ours since Christ suffered and his virgins have been ready to die in defence of their chastity. I shall make no reference to the persons who inflict such suffering, for where the Lord's grace is the Lord's peace should be too. I do not come here to make public accusation against anybody; I am simply defending myself against the accusation that has been made. I have reason to think that most of my accusers are here listening to me. I want to refute their ideas, not to reveal their identity. The gist of their accusation is that I encourage chastity. Anyone who now opposes that counsel of mine will *ipso facto* reveal himself.

Ambrose defends the celibate state

25. "You stress the idea of virginity," runs the charge, "and you succeed in persuading many people." I wish I were really and truly convinced of this fine accusation and that my results really proved it. Opposition would hold no terrors for

me if only I could feel that my efforts had such success. I only wish you could convict me by facts instead of striking me with empty words. I fear that the accusations may lack substance and merely result in bringing me praise that I do not deserve.

26. Their accusation continues: "Once girls are initiated into the sacred mysteries, they make a promise of virginity, and you forbid them to marry ever after." I wish in fact I could also get in the way of those others who are on the threshold of matrimony; I wish I could change their bridal veil. What on earth is wrong with my refusal to let consecrated virgins be pulled away from their altars into matrimony? If they have free choice of a life-partner, may they not choose God? The repute of my endeavour has been turned upside down: it brings me dishonor, though always in the past the priestly office has been proud to scatter the seeds of chastity and promote love of virginity.

27. I am eager to find out the exact reason for the accusation. Is it that my idea is wrong? Or new-fangled? Or useless? If I am just wrong, then so are the vows I praise, so is the very life of the angels, which the glory of our resurrection will imitate: "When the dead rise again there is no marrying and giving in marriage; they are as the angels in heaven are" (Mt 20:30). He who condemns virginity condemns our desire for that resurrection. Resurrection can hardly be counted wrong if it is assigned as the final reward for mankind; and its likeness, virginity, can hardly be offensive if its model is approved both by present desire and by future enjoyment.

The pursuit of chastity

28. Assuming then that there is nothing wrong about it, how is it new-fangled? I am all for condemning any novelties that

Christ did not teach, for Christ is the one and only right road for the believer. If Christ did not teach what I teach, then I am quite ready to admit that my doctrine is detestable. Let us sort out the matter. Did Christ recommend chastity? Or did he disown it? What he said was: "Some have made themselves eunuchs for love of the kingdom of heaven" (Mt 19:12). This means that there is a gallant soldiery which fights for the kingdom of heaven; the Lord taught that the pursuit of chastity should be inviolate.

29. The Apostles, seeing chastity's superiority over everything else, said: "If the case stands so between man and wife it is better not to marry at all" (Mt 19:10). They obviously regarded the burdens of marriage as heavy ones and showed preference for the grace of true integrity. The Lord knew that purity is preached to the many but practiced by the few, and he said: "That conclusion cannot be taken in by everybody" (Mt 19:11). He meant that chastity is not a common thing, not something for the crowd, not something permitted because of infirmity but given in view of virtue. When he said, "Some have made themselves eunuchs for love of the kingdom of heaven," he meant that this was a matter for exceptional virtue, for he added: "Take this in, you whose hearts are large enough for it" (Mt 19:12).

30. Just after that statement children were brought to him for his blessing. These children, yet ignorant of evil, possessed in their innocence the gift of purity. He said: "The kingdom of heaven belongs to such as these," belongs to people who return to the purity of childhood, to a childlike ignorance of corruption. Virginity has received its approval in those heavenly words; it is recommended by the precepts of our Lord.

31. Let us follow the teaching of that divine voice. He had previously said that marriage was not to be broken "except in the case of fornication"; but he mentioned in the same context the grace and gift of integrity, to show that, though marriage is to be approved and not condemned, the cult of integrity nevertheless is preferable. Nobody then could be so averse to truth as to decry marriage. Yet who could be so unreasonable as to overlook the burdens of wedlock? "A woman who is free of wedlock, or a virgin, is concerned with the Lord's claim, intent on holiness, bodily and spiritual; whereas the married woman is concerned with the world's claim, asking how she is to please her husband" (1 Cor 7:34).

The chains of wedlock

32. Alongside these preoccupations of marriage, though the state implies no sin, there will be sorrows of the flesh, such as the heavy labor of childbirth and all the trouble of bearing and educating children. Paul in advance laid down the rule that no one should be deterred by these troubles. In the pains of childbirth, many women are all for giving up marriage. Men too sometimes shirk the onus of married life and cease to love their wives. This the Apostle forestalled: "Art thou yoked to a wife? Then do not go about to free thyself" (1 Cor 7:27). I like that word "yoked": Man and wife are coupled together by a yoke of affection and are linked to each other in a harness of love.

33. The chains of wedlock are golden. But they are chains all the same. This good yoke is a very real one, a worldly one, that of trying to please a man rather than God. Even the wounds of charity are good and are preferable to kisses. "Better the love that scourges than hate's false kiss" (Prov 27:6). Peter wounds with the sword, Judas kisses; the kiss

condemns the one, the wound corrects the other. In the kisses of Judas is the poison of betrayal, in the tears of Peter the cleansing of sin. To show from the prophet's words the goodness of the wound of charity the Church quotes "I am lovesick all the while" (Song 2:5).

34. No one then whose choice is marriage must blame virginity and no one who follows virginity must condemn marriage. The Church has censured long ago those who dare to abolish the marriage bond. Listen to the Church's words: "Come with me, my true love; for us the country ways, the cottage roof for shelter. Dawn shall find us in the vineyard, looking to see what flowers has the vine" (Song 7:11). The countryside grows many fruits, but the best field always has flowers as well as fruit, and the Church is such a field, rich with diverse growth. You will see the saplings of virginity in spring flower here, you will find widowhood richly fruitful there; in another part the Church's harvest of marriage fills the world's granaries with ripe grain, fills the winepress of Christ with the abundant fruit of faithful wedlock.

35. The pursuit of chastity is therefore neither wrong nor novel. Can it perhaps be thought devoid of utility? I have heard people say that because of it the world has collapsed, the race has declined, marriage has come to an end. I ask them: have you seen any man looking for a wife without being able to find one? When has a dispute ever taken place, or a man lost his life, over a nun? From marriage on the other hand, wars do arise, to kill the adulterer, or to hound down the woman-snatcher. Those are the real struggles that damage the state. No one has ever suffered penalty because a virgin was consecrated, for chastity does not need to enforce penalties; it arises from devotion and is preserved by faith.

Why virginity supports marriage

36. If anybody still thinks that the human race is diminished by the profession of chastity, let him consider that where those are few, people are few, and where virginity flourishes the population is large. Think of all those girls in the churches of Alexandria, in the East and in Africa, who make their profession every year. Fewer births take place here than profession ceremonies there! So, the practice of the whole wide world warrants the judgment that virginity is not useless to society. Remember that through a virgin, salvation came to regenerate the whole Roman world.

37. If someone wants to prevent virginity, he should also forbid wives to remain continent. In that way he would cause more frequent childbirth. He should let no wife remain faithful while her husband is absent from home; after all, she ought not diminish the possibility of offspring or let slip by the years best suited to motherhood.

38. It is objected that young men are finding it difficult to get wives. Actually, it may be much easier than they think. I want to get in touch with those people who think virginity ought to be proscribed for this reason. Who exactly are these people? Are they married or unmarried? If married, they have no need for alarm, for they no longer need the girls consecrated to virginity to be their wives. If unmarried, they must not do themselves the injury of pinning all their hopes on such girls as have no desire to marry. Is it fathers who object, anxious about a match for their daughters and set against the dedication of virginity? These fathers if they are wise need have no fears, for with fewer girls on the scene their daughters will soon be off their hands.

39. Many say that girls should be older than at present when they take the veil. I admit that a bishop must guard against

letting a girl take the veil rashly. He ought to take account of her age, I mean the age of her faith and modesty. Let him look for the maturity of modesty, the grey hairs of wisdom, the old age of good behavior, the years of purity, the spirit of chastity. He should also see to it that her mother's care is safe and her choice of company industrious and serious. If these conditions are present the virgin will not be lacking in age. If they are not present the girl should be sent away; she is too young in character, whatever her age.

40. What must be examined is not her youth but her disposition. Thecla was tested not by age but by virtue. I need not dwell on this point; every age of life is fit for God and perfect for union with Christ. Virtue is not a consequence of age but *vice versa.* There is nothing wonderful about young girls making their profession when you read about martyrdom in the case of children. The Scripture in fact says: "Thou hast made the lips of children, of infants at the breast, vocal with praise" (Ps 8:3). No doubt, but youth can follow Christ to continence when infancy can follow him to martyrdom. Do we think it incredible that young women now follow Christ to his kingdom when children once followed him to the desert? You remember how four thousand men were fed with five loaves, "not reckoning', says the text, "women and children" (Mt 14:21).

Disposition counts more than youth

41. So do not keep the little ones away from Christ, for little ones have suffered martyrdom for him. "The kingdom of heaven belongs to such as these" (Mt 19:13). If the Lord calls them, are you going to keep them away? He said: "Do not keep them back from me" (Mt 19:14). Do not keep back those young maidens of whom it is written: "What

wonder the maids should love thee?" (Song 1:3). Do not separate children from the love of Christ, for a child while still in his mother's womb confessed Christ with prophetic joy (Lk 1:14).

42. At the very beginning of the Church crowds went after Christ. What prompted them? "Because," says the Gospel, "he laid his hands upon them and healed them" (Lk 4:40). He never had a fixed time or place for healing; everywhere and always his cure would be administered. It was at home Mary was greeted by the angel (Lk 1:28), at home David was anointed prophet (1 Kings 16:13). But Jesus tends and cures everywhere: on the highway, in houses, away in the desert. On a journey he cured the woman who touched the hem of his garment (Mt 9:20). In a house he raised to life the daughter of a leader of the synagogue (Mt 5:41). In the desert a whole crowd was healed. Listen to the description. "When the sun was going down all those who had friends afflicted with diseases of any kind brought them to him; and he laid his hands upon each one of them and healed them." In the desert at sunset, he healed by the laying on of his hands, showing himself at once God and man. Naturally the crowd was after him again the next morning.

43. I see order in these events. At sunset the sick are brought to him and at dawn the crowds come out looking for him. When can Christ be sought? Only in the day. He who walks in the light will not depart from Christ. Night heard the groans of the sick, but day saw the faith of the people and the joy of the healed. What was written is fulfilled: "Sorrow is but the guest of a night and joy comes in the morning" (Ps 30:5). There could be no greater joy for the crowd than to follow Christ even into the desert.

44. His conduct teaches us that the aspirant to perfection must shun vain glory. He never objected to the great number of the sick but he shunned all ostentation in what he did. We, too, if we desire to be saved or deserve to be healed, must keep away from soft living, away from licentiousness, and with parched body follow Christ in his flight from pleasure along the dry and fruitless desert of this life.

45. We must follow him in the daytime. The day of the Church is at hand, the day which Abraham saw with joy. Let us follow Christ during that day, for he is not to be found in the night. "In the night watches, as I lay abed, I searched for my heart's love, and searched in vain" (Song 3:1).

Warning about public places

46. Christ is not found in the marketplace or in the streets. (See #88 for a fuller explanation.") He was not found in such places by her whose resolve was "to stir abroad and traverse the city, searching every alleyway and street for him I love so tenderly. But for all my search I could not find him" (Song 3:2). Let us not seek Christ where we have no chance of finding him. Christ is not a man-about-town. Christ is peace, but the forum is for dispute. Christ is justice but the forum is for iniquity. Christ is a worker, and the forum is for empty idleness. Christ is charity but, in the forum, there is malice. Christ is fidelity, the forum means deception and treachery. Christ is in the Church but in the forum, there are idols. The widow whom I took to task in a previous book of mine *[de viduis]* for her mundane habits can now see that my words were not meant as invective but as advice and that I was being more solicitous than sharp-tongued; in a spirit of reconciliation let her note what I say: in the Church the widow receives justice but, in the forum, she is led astray. Let us shun the marketplace, let us get away from the streets.

47. "Hail discernment as thy friend. So, wilt thou learn to shun the temptress with her honeyed words, the wife that is no wife of thine, . . . ere now looking down from her window through the lattice" (Prov 7:4–6). We must avoid the streets. It is harmful not to find there the Christ you are seeking; it is harmful too to search in places where you ought not. To seek Christ in the houses of men, just because they pretend to the title of teachers, is to be brazen rather than modest.

48. After the Church's example we must be careful not to get caught by the watchmen who go about the city. The Church's words are: "As they went the city rounds, the watchmen fell in with me, that guard the walls; beat me and left me wounded and took away my cloak" (Song 5:7). My daughters, the Church's wounds come not to herself but to us. We must be careful then not to let our lapses be a wound to the Church, not to let anybody take away our cloak, that is, the garment of prudence and the uniform of patience. These virtues replace all desire for soft garments: "You must look in the kings' palaces for men that go clad in silk" (Mt 11:8). Christ gave us the cloak in which he clothed himself and his apostles. When he tells you that if a man wants your coat, you should let him have your cloak too (Mt 5:40), he means that you should give the man your philosopher's robe and clothe him in that garment of prudence.

Seek Christ where the Church seeks him.

49. Daughters, we must seek Christ in the same place where the Church seeks him, that is, on the mountains of good fragrance. These mountains, the heights of good deeds, exhale the sweet fragrance of holiness from their pinnacles of merit. Christ flees from the streets, the meeting places of men, and

the noise of the marketplace, according to what is written: "Thy bridegroom with thee, hasten away like gazelle or fawn that spurns the scented hill underfoot" (Song 8:14). An object of hate to the snakes that crawl on the earth, fleeing the haunts of what lies low, an enemy of reptiles, he cannot live except on the heights of the virtues. He cannot dwell except among those daughters of the Church who are able to say: "We are Christ's incense offered to God" (2 Cor 21:15). The odor of death attaches to those who are on the road to death, but life-giving perfume to those whose vivid faith exhales the Lord's resurrection.

50. Those are the mountains of spices which received the body of the Lord Jesus, bound "in winding cloth with spices" (Jn 19:40). Those who have believed that Jesus died, was buried and rose again, have reached the high summit of faith with its pinnacles of virtue. Where, then, are we to look for Christ? In the prudence of the priestly heart.

51. We have said that Christ is to be sought in the desert. He himself gives us yet another direction: "Wild rose on the lowland plain, wild lily on the mountain slopes, a lily among the brambles" (Song 2:1–2). In that, you have another place where the Lord likes to pass his time; in fact, not just one place but several. "Wild rose of the plain": he frequents the open simplicity of a pure mind. "Wild lily on the mountain slopes": the flower of Christ is the flower of lowliness, not of rich living, not of pleasures, not of wantonness; rather, the flower of simplicity, the flower of humility. "A lily among the brambles": is it not among the roughness of hard labor and sorrow of soul that the flower of sweetest perfume grows? God is appeased by a heart of sorrow.

52. This is the desert, my daughters, which leads to a kingdom. This also is the desert which blooms like the lily, according to

what is written down: "Thrills the barren desert with rejoicing; the wilderness takes heart and blossoms fair as the lily" (Is 35:1). In that desert, daughters, the good tree is fruitful; it brings forth fruit that is wholesome, spreads wide the branches of its good deeds, and its top reaches up into the divine. Close to it all others are fruitful, for the writing is: "As an apple tree in the wild woodland, such is he my heart longs for, matched with his fellows" (Song 2:3). At this the Church may rejoice and say in her joy: "Shade cool to rest under, fruit sweet to the taste" (Song 2:3).

53. Yes, the Church, rejoicing at the results of our faith, may say: "Lead me into the banquet-hall, set in battle-order my love." (Song 2:4) Love cannot exist without faith, for the Church has three securities: hope, faith, and charity. When hope leads, and faith is firmly founded, love is set in order, and the Church is united.

54. You have learned, then, where you may look for Christ. Now learn too how you are to induce him to come looking for you. Rouse up the Holy Spirit, saying (Cant. 4.16): "North wind, awake; wind of the south, awake and come; blow through this garden of mine and set its fragrance all astir. Into his garden then let my true love come and taste his fruit." The garden of the Word is the blossoming love of the devout soul and the fruit in the garden is virtue.

55. So he comes. Whether you eat or whether you drink, so long as you invoke Christ, he will come to you, saying (Prov 9:5): "Come and eat at my table, come and drink of the wine I have brewed for you." Even when you are asleep, he comes and knocks at your door, comes and puts his hand through the window. But he does not always come; and he does not come to everybody, but only to that soul which can say, "Ah, but my shift (garment) I have laid it by in the night."

(Song 5:3). In the night of this world, you must put off, like a garment, the life of the flesh. Remember that the Lord himself put off his garment of flesh that he might triumph for you over the dominations and powers of this world.

56. (Song 5:3): "I have laid it by; how can I put it on again?" That is what the soul devoted to God says. She so puts off the mundane acts of the body that she would no longer know how to put them on again if she so wished. 'How can I put it on again?': with what dread, with what shame, with what memories? The new habit of good does away completely with the old habit of imperfection.

The symbolism of washing the feet

57. (Song 5:3): "My feet I washed but now; shall I soil them with the dust?" You know from the Gospel that washing the feet means the mystery of faith, and is a mark of humility. The Gospel (Jn 13:14) says: "Why then if I have washed your feet, I who am the master and the Lord, you in your turn ought to wash each other's feet." There, you see the humility. As for the mystery, a person must wash his feet if he wishes to have his share with Christ, who says (Jn13:8): "If I do not wash you, it means that you have no companionship with me." If this was said about Peter, it certainly fits us.

58. He who washes his feet will not want to wash them again, and so he must beware of soiling them. Well then does the Church say: "My feet I washed but now." She does not say: "How shall I wash them again?" but: "Shall I soil them again in the dust?" As if she had forgotten all about the old stain, all about former soiling. In a corporal action she shows us how we ought to wash away all traces of stain on the soul. So then when you have washed your feet in the stream of the eternal font, and have cleansed them in the sacramental

mysteries, take care that they are not soiled again by corporal desires or by the earthly stains of bad actions.

59. Those are the feet which David washed in the spirit. He shows you too how you must not soil yours again, for he says (Ps 122:2): "In thy gates, Jerusalem, our feet stand at last." Here, of course, you must think not of bodily feet but of those of the soul; how indeed could one of earth stand with bodily feet in heaven? Jerusalem, as you know from Paul, is Heaven. He taught you how you may stand in heaven when he said (Phil 3:20): "We find our true home in heaven," that is, the home of our actions and habits, the home of our deeds, the home of our faith.

60. Whoever lives like this can say (Song 5:4–5): "Then my true love thrust his head through the lattice, and I trembled inwardly at his touch. I rose to let him in." It is good if our heart is disturbed at the approach of the Lord. If Mary was disturbed at the approach of an angel how much more may we be disturbed at the coming of Christ? When divine things come upon us, corporal affection goes away and the habit of the exterior man ceases. Be disturbed, then, and hasten. The Israelites were commanded to eat the paschal lamb in haste. Rise quickly then and open the door, for Christ is there; he is knocking at the entrance of your house. If you only open it, he will come in and the Father will be with him.

61. It is not only when he has come in that he gives his treasure. He gives it in advance. Beforehand the soul experiences disturbance, and feeling her way along the walls of her home, seeks the door of Christ. She undoes the bolts of the flesh, opens the house of the body, as Christ knocks on the doors. (Song 5:5): "My hands dripped ever with myrrh; still with the choicest myrrh my fingers were slippery as I caught the latch."

The myrrh which drips from the hands of the soul is that of the just man Nicodemus, that master in Israel, who first heard of the mystery of purification and brought his mixture of myrrh and aloes, about a hundred pounds weight, to anoint the body of Jesus. He brought the perfect perfume of his faith.

62. This perfume is breathed by the soul which prepares to open to Christ and is the first to receive the fragrance of the Lord's burial, believing that his flesh has not seen corruption, has not withered in death. Embalmed in the perfume of that eternal flower, it rises unwithered. How could there be a withering in his flesh when his name means "ointment poured." He poured himself out that his perfume might breathe upon you.

The perfume of faith

63. This perfume always existed, but only with the Father and in the Father. His fragrance was known only to the angels and archangels, kept within the vessel of heaven. But the Father said (Is 49:6): "I have appointed thee to be the light of the Gentiles, in thee I will send out my salvation to the furthest corners of the earth." The Son descended; things were filled with the new perfume of the Word; the heart of the Father "uttered a good word"; the Son exhaled divine fragrance; the Spirit spread his fragrance abroad among all hearts. (Rom 5:5): "The love of God has been poured out in our hearts by the Holy Spirit whom we have received."

64. At first the Son of God kept his perfume in the vase of his body, awaiting his time, as he said (Is 50:4): "Ever the Lord schools my tongue to utterance; awakes my dull ears . . . their master's bidding to heed." The hour came and he opened his mouth; with that perfume, virtue went out from him.

65. This perfume was poured out over the Jews and was collected by the Gentiles; it was poured in the land of Judaea, but its fragrance reached all the world. With this perfume Mary was anointed; as virgin she conceived, as virgin brought forth the good odor, the Son of God. This perfume was poured out over the waters and sanctified them. With it the three youths were anointed and then the very flames rained moisture for them. With it too, Daniel was anointed and pacified the fierce mouths of the lions.

66. This perfume flows out daily, never diminished. Take your vessel, virgin; draw near and be filled with this unguent. Accept the ointment valued at three hundred *denarii* but given free; all may have it without cost. Virgin, anoint yourself with it. Do not have Judas's sadness at the pouring of it. Rather let it give burial to Christ in you. And then close your vessel that the perfume may not flow from it. Close it, I say, with the stopper of purity, of modesty in speech, of abstinence from vainglory.

67. She who has this unguent has Christ and can say (Song 5:6): "When I opened, my true love was gone; he had passed me by." How had he passed? He had passed through the inner places of the mind, as in the case of Mary (Lk 2:35): "As for thy own soul, it shall have a sword to pierce it." For the word of God is alive, and like a sharp sword it penetrates and pierces the joints of bodily thoughts and the inner things of the heart.

Adornment with virtues

68. You, soul, are one of the people, one of the plebes; Christ does not marvel at any of the distinctions of secular pomp such as costly garments or precious necklaces or expensive

garlands glittering with gems, the expense of which often causes dispute in the church and loss of peace. Yes, you are one who illumines the beauty of your body with the light of your mind. You are even more fit to be compared with the Church. In the hours of the night, think always upon Christ, and hope for his coming at every moment.

69. If he seems to you to be slow in coming, rise up. He seems to delay when you stay too long in sleep, when you cease from prayer, when you do not raise your voice in psalms. Give the first fruits of your vigils to Christ, give him the first fruit of your actions. You heard me say a while ago that he calls you (Song 4:8): "Venture forth from Lebanon, and come to me, my bride, my queen that shall be. "You will pass over to Christ to fight against the world; you will cross to him, triumphing over the world. You have heard that he has separated you from the attacks of lions and leopards, which mean spiritual enemies. You have heard that the beauty of your virtues pleases him, you have heard that he loves above all others the perfume of your garments, the fragrance of integrity. You have heard that you are a garden sealed, filled with the sweet fruit of good trees. Ask then for the Holy Spirit to breathe upon you and give you the fragrance of piety and spiritual grace. He will reply to you (Song 5:2): "I lie asleep; but oh, my heart is wakeful."

70. You hear the voice of one knocking at the door and saying (Song 5:2): "Let me in, my true love, so gentle; my bride, so pure." True love in charity, gentle as the dove, perfect in purity. "See how bedewed is my head, how the night rains have drenched my hair." (Song 5:2). As the dew from heaven removes the drought of the night, so the dew of Our Lord Jesus Christ distils the moisture of eternal life in the darkness of the world. He is the bedewed head, untouched by

the drought of the world. The Scripture says (Lk 23:31) “If it goes hard with the tree that is still green, what will become of the tree that is already dried up?” This head is rich with dew for itself and for others. Your head is Christ, ever abundant, never drained by his own liberality, never impoverished by long generosity. To this head was never raised the helmet of strife and discord.

71. Now consider carefully that it is not ordinary dew that is mentioned in the words (Song 5:2): “How the night rains have drenched my hair!” And do not, my dear sister, think that the reference is to material curls. These are not an adornment but a condemnation. They are a vain display of looks, not a school of virtue. Different are the curls of the Nazarite, untouched by the iron, clipped by no one, not arranged by iron tongs, or decked out by art, but twisted in a sheen of manifold virtue. The Bible will tell you about these locks which, kept intact, rendered Samson invincible (Judg 16:17), until they were cut, and he lost his strength.

72. On hearing the voice of the Word do not seek the garment you took off, to put it on again. You may all too easily find it, or it may be offered to you by the evil spirit. Forget it, forget how to put it on. As if the Lord were at hand free yourself from bodily ties and rise trembling. As you rise prepare the inner mind for prayer, that you may hasten from the things below to the things on high; see how to open the doors of your heart. As you stretch out your hands to Christ, their deeds will exhale the fragrance of fidelity.

Pleasure arises from the heart

73. Raise your hands then to your nostrils and examine the fragrance of your deeds with keen attention. The fragrance of your right hand will soothe you; your body will be redolent of

the perfume of the resurrection. Your fingers will drip with myrrh; your spiritual deeds will be fragrant with the grace of true faith. Your pleasure then will lie in the depth of your own heart; you will be your own sweet source of pleasure. You will bring yourself none of the dissatisfaction that often comes to sinners for you will keep drawing more and more delight from a pure inner simplicity, denuded of all the deceitful outer trappings of the flesh.

74. That is as Christ has desired you and chosen you. And so, he enters at the open door. He will not fail to do so, for he has promised to enter. Embrace him whom you have sought. Approach him and be illumined. Hold him and ask him not to go away quickly. Beg him not to depart. For the Word of God runs and will not be held by the world. You have heard that he has separated you from the attacks of lions and leopards, which mean spiritual enemies. You have heard that the beauty of your virtues pleases him, you have heard that he loves above all others the perfume of your garments, the good fragrance of integrity. You have heard that you are a garden sealed, filled with the sweet fruit of good trees. Ask then for the Holy Spirit to breathe upon you and give you the fragrance of piety and spiritual grace. He will reply to you (Song 5:2): "I lie asleep; but oh, my heart is wakeful."

75. What does she say next? (Song 5:6): "And now I searched for him in vain; there was no answer when I called out to him." Because he has gone past so quickly, do not think that you are displeasing to him, for you have called him, asked him, opened to him. He allows us to be tired. When the crowds asked him not to depart, did he not say (Luke 4:43): "I must preach the gospel of God's kingdom to the other cities too; it is for this that I was sent"? Even if he does seem to have left you, go out, look for him again.

How to find Christ

76. Devoted then to God, do not fear those guards who stand round the door; do not fear those who go about the city; do not fear their wounds, for no wounds can come to those who follow Christ. Even if they take away the life of your body, Christ is still at hand. When you have found him, know how to dwell with him, that he may not have to leave you. He is quick to desert those who are careless.

77. Nobody can teach you better than the Church herself how you are to keep Christ with you. In fact, if you have followed the Scripture reading, she has already told you (Song 3:4): "Then when I had scarce left them, I found him so tenderly loved; and now that he is mine I will never leave him, never let him go." With what ties is Christ to be held? Not by force, not by chains, but rather by the bonds of charity. He is kept and held by the ties of the mind, by the love of the heart. So, if you want to hold Christ, seek him continually and fear no penalty. It is often in pain of the body, amid the very hands of persecutors, that Christ may really be found. "When I had scarce left them, I found him." In a little while, in a moment, when you have escaped the hands of your persecutors and have not succumbed to the powers of the world, Christ will meet you and will allow you to be tempted no further.

78. She who seeks Christ and finds him can say (Song 3:4): "I will never leave him, never let him go until I have brought him into my own mother's house, into the room that saw my birth." What is this mother's house, this room that saw birth, except the inner secret of your own person? Keep this home, cleanse the inner chambers of this dwelling, so that when the house is all pure, unstained by sinful conscience, your spiritual home may stand as a priestly temple, built upon its cornerstone, with the Spirit dwelling in it. She who thus seeks

and entreats Christ is never abandoned, but visited by him frequently, for he stays (Mt 28:20) "until the consummation of the world."

79. That is the way to find and hold Christ who puts his hand through your window. This window is the eye of the soul, the vision of the mind, through which we see the works of Christ. Virgin, let Christ enter through your lattice, let Christ put his hand through it; let there come through it the love of the Word, not that of the body. But if the Word puts his hand through your window, make sure to prepare it, make sure to remove every speck of the dust of sin. Let there be no stain there, no sin in the virgin's window. Away with cosmetics, and all the other trifles of faked beauty. Away with those enticements of adulterous love. The same applies to the ears: they are to have no weights suspended from them, no wounds inflicted on them, and their only adornment must be to listen to what is edifying.

80. Learn also how to close your door in the hours of the night. Nobody must find it open. Your spouse wishes to find that door closed when he comes to knock. The door is the mouth, and to Christ only must it be opened. It must be opened only when the word of God has first knocked upon it. So, it is written (Song 4:12): "My bride, my true love, a close garden; hedged all about, a spring shut in and sealed." This implies that the mouth must not easily open, must not break its seal in vulgar conversation. You should not open it even to speak of divine things, except when you give your responses to the Word of God. As you have no business with others, speak only to Christ, hold conversation only with him. For if "women are to be silent in the churches, utterance is not permitted to them" (1 Cor 14:34), with even more reason must your door be closed, the gate of the widow

be shut fast. All too swiftly the enemy of modesty can creep into your speech and words will escape you, which you would dearly wish to recall.

The power of a chaste soul

81. If Eve had kept her door closed Adam would not have been deceived, for she would not have answered the queries of the serpent. Death entered through that lattice of Eve's lips. Death will enter too through your door if you speak falsely, if you speak basely, if you speak immodestly, if you speak out of place. Let the door of your lips be closed; in the porch of your voice see that the bolt is pressed home. Draw that bolt only when you hear the voice of God, the word of God.

82. Then myrrh will drip for you, the grace of baptism will breathe upon you; that with Christ you may die to this world and with him rise again (Col 2:20): "Why do you live by these prescriptions, as if the world were still your element? Prescriptions against touching or tasting or handling those creatures which vanish altogether as we enjoy them, all based on the will and the word of men?" Corruption ought to be far away from the chaste. Bury then, all care of the flesh and of the world (Col 3:1). Risen with Christ, you must lift up your thoughts to where Christ now sits. Seeking Christ means seeing God the Father, for Christ sits at his right hand.

83. She who seeks Christ should not be seen with the common mob, should not be found in the marketplace or on the streets, should not be loud-voiced, or unguarded in deportment, or ready to hear everything and be seen everywhere. The Apostle forbids you earthly conversation and orders you, beyond the limits of nature, to fly to heaven with spiritual wings. He says (Col 3:2): "You must be heavenly-minded,

not earthly-minded." This is impossible to us while we are in this cloister of the body. When the body dies, the soul can take to flying back to the things above, but while we live it is tied down by the law of nature. Paul therefore added: "You have undergone death; and your life is hidden away now with Christ in God." If it is so hidden with Christ in God, let it not appear in the eyes of the world; Christ is dead to the world and lives to God.

84. See now how Christ likes to be desired and does not like empty conversation. The virgin who opened her door to the word of God said (Song 5:6): "He had passed me by, how my heart had melted at the sound of his voice!" Her heart had left the world, left this life, and stayed with Christ. "And now I searched for him in vain." Christ indeed loves to be long sought after.

85. "The keepers of the walls found her." (Song 3:3) Perhaps different kinds of keepers are to be understood here, for this city does not close the gates in its walls, as we read (Rev 21:25): "All day the gates will never be shut (there will be no night there), as the nations flock into it with their honor and their praise." That is the city of Jerusalem which is in heaven, within which you are kept perfect and immaculate, for nothing common enters into it. Chastity and modesty are not common things; they are written in the book of life.

86. If we find the city, we must enter it. We must see its lights, see its walls, see its citizens, see the foundations, see too the keepers of the walls. But how are we to enter? There is one way which leads to life, and that way is Christ; then let us follow Christ. This city is in heaven. How are we to ascend there? The Evangelist tells how (Rev 21:10): "And he carried me off in a trance to a great mountain, high up, and there showed me the holy city, Jerusalem, as it came down, sent by

God, from heaven." Let us ascend there in the spirit because flesh cannot ascend to it. Let us be on our way towards heaven now, that the city may come down to us, the city with light like precious stones, jasper and crystal, the city that has a great and high wall.

87. As well as the light and the wall, let us think of the gates and the guards. (Rev 21:12): "With twelve gates and twelve angels at the gates, and the names of the twelve tribes of Israel carved on the lintels." On the gates the names of the patriarchs are written, on the walls those of the Apostles. The Apostles are the foundations of the city; and the cornerstone is Christ, on which the whole structure is built. God without, God within, God everywhere. The city has the majesty of God. You, holy virgins, and all others who are just and immaculate of soul, are fellow citizens of the saints, domestics of God. You will possess that noble fatherhood if you seek Christ within its confines, if you enter it by faith and good deeds, if you are illumined by the light of the patriarchs, built upon the Apostles, holding converse with angels.

The cloak of the chaste

88. How can the keepers be angels, if they take away the cloak of the chaste soul? Remember that the cloak of the virgin is different from that of the girl who frequents the town. She who seeks Christ in the marketplace loses the cloak which she possessed, for prudence is not retained in the marketplace or in the streets but only in the Church. Still, I should like to find favor with all such people and tell them that the Lord is merciful to everybody, and that they also may find Christ if they seek him continually; perhaps the cloak may merely mean the garment of the body.

89. The person therefore who seeks Christ in the chamber should seek like him who said (Ps 63:6): "My thoughts shall go out to thee at dawn"; the seeking should go on in the night, according to the writing (Ps 134:2): "At midnight lift up your hands towards the sanctuary." The search must be in the city, in the marketplace, and on the streets: in the city, that is, of our God; in the marketplace where sits the Judge of divine law; in the streets from which were collected those who came to the Lord's supper. By keeping up that search one may meet the angels who are keepers of the city of God.

90. From the heavenly nature of the keepers we can see that the city is heavenly. The marketplace is the heavenly one of eternal justice; the streets are not common ones, but those perhaps in which that fountain flows of which we read (Prov 5:16): "Like waters from thine own fountains, flowing through the public streets." Seeking Christ there you meet the angels.

91. But if we reach the angels by our merits, why is the one who arrives wounded by them? Because there is a good sword, and it deals a good wound, the word of God wounds without slaying. This is the wound of good love, of charity, described in (Song 5:7–8): "Wounded by love all the while." She who is perfect is wounded by love. The wounds of the Word are good, those of the lover (Prov 27:6): "Better the love that scourges, than hate's false kiss." Rebecca (Gen 24:58) was wounded by love when leaving her parents and going to her spouse. Rachel (Gen 30:1) was so wounded, when she was troubled over her sister and loved Jacob. Barren herself, she envied her sister because of her many children. She was a type of the Church to whom is said: (Is 54:1): "Sing with praise, barren city that art childless still; echo thy praise, cry aloud, wife that was never brought to bed."

92. So the keepers, on finding her, wounded her and took away her cloak. They took the cloak of corporal deeds so that in pure simplicity of mind she might seek Christ. One clad only in the garment of philosophy, that garb of worldly wisdom, cannot see Christ. It is well then that she loses the cloak of philosophy, for thus no one will lead her astray through philosophy. It is good to be robbed of her cloak in approaching Christ; with a pure heart she may now go and see God (Mt 5:7): "Blessed are the clean of heart; they shall see God." When her heart has been cleansed, she can find the Word, she can see God.

93. Seek him then and let us all seek him. Soul is not confined to one sex, though it is named in the feminine gender, perhaps because it is subject to the affections of the body but can calm the movements of the flesh with sweetness and affection.

94. By prayers and beseeching we ought to invite God to breathe upon us like a gentle wind from the south, the air of the Word. This wind hurts none of the fruit trees but enlivens them with its gentle blowing. It is written (Song 1:9): "I compare you, my love, to a mare of Pharaoh's chariots." (RSVCE) We know from *Numbers* that Aminadab was the father of Nasson, who was a prince of the people of Judah. As such he was a figure of Christ who is true head of his people and guides the chariot of the just soul with the reins of the Word, keeping the fury of its spirited horses from crashing headlong.

The four spirited horses

95. The horses are the four affections of the soul: anger, cupidity, pleasure, fear. When these are active the soul loses herself under the weight of the corruptible body. The

body, like a chariot drawn by untamed animals, drags her along unwillingly, tossed by vain cares, until such time as these passions grow calm in the power of the Word. The Word, as a good charioteer, takes care that the soul, itself immortal, may not have a difficult course when joined to the mortal body.

96. The first task is to tame these swift motions of the body and bridle them with the rein of reason. Then care must be taken that irregular motion does not cause entanglement as happens with horses; often the good horse is buried by the bad, the swift held up by the slow, the tame upset by the unruly. The bad horse neighs and leaps, damaging the chariot or overloading his companion. This animal must be soothed by the good charioteer and guided into the track of truth, avoiding the deviations of falsehood. The road upwards is safe; the descending road is dangerous. Those who have successfully carried the yoke of the Word are led to the manger of the Lord in which their food is not bodily fodder but the Bread which descends from heaven.

97. The wheels of this chariot are those spoken of by the prophet (Ezek 1:20): "The wheels had a living impulse in them." The chariot of the soul, being smooth and well-shaped, runs freely.

98. But I must not digress further. The Word of God is invited down into the garden in which there is the fruit of sacred reading and priestly grace, bitter with temptation, hard with labor, but abundant in inner virtues. The rod of Aaron blossomed, not by its own nature but by secret power. The Word comes down into the garden that he may reap the harvest of faith, catch its odors, find heavenly food, and enjoy the sweetness of our honey (Song 5:1): "Myrrh and spices of mine all reaped; the honey eaten in

its comb, the wine drunk and the milk that were kept for me." This honey is gathered from the varied flowers of virtue, in harmonious labor, by the bees that are models of wisdom. The Church keeps this honey in her combs as food for Christ.

99. Christ means everything to us. Each soul ought to go to him, whether sick with bodily sins, or nailed down by some desire of the world, or still imperfect but desiring to advance in prayer, or even perfect perhaps in many virtues. Each must approach him, for all our power is in his hands and he is all things to us. If you want your wound cured, he is the physician. If you burn with fever, he is a cool fountain. If you are weighed down by iniquity, he is justice. If you need help, he is power. If you fear death, he is life. If you desire heaven, he is the way there. If you flee the darkness, he is the light. If you seek food, he is the nourishment. (Ps 34:9): "How gracious the Lord is! Taste and prove it; blessed is the man that learns to trust in him."

100. The woman with the issue of blood trusted in him and at once she was healed because of the faith with which she approached. You too, my daughter, touch the hem of his garment. The flow of worldly passion will be dried up in the abundant heat of the saving Word. But you must approach with faith, and with devotion grasp the hem of the divine Word. You must fall humbly at his feet. And where are the feet of the Word except where is the body of Christ? O faith, richer than all treasures, stronger than all power of the body, more health-giving than all medicine! As soon as the woman approached him, she felt his power and received his healing. If you turn your eye towards the light, it is illuminated before you feel anything, for the action of light precedes your sensation. The woman's long-standing malady, that could not

be healed by the skill of medical art or by any expense, was cured by the mere touch of Christ's clothing. Virgin, imitate that woman in the modesty of her approach and in the fervor of her faith.

101. Notice the grace that was given her; previously she had been ashamed to be seen, but now she was not ashamed to confess her defect. Do not try to conceal your lapses but confess them to the Lord who already knows them. Do not be ashamed of confessing, for the Prophets were not ashamed. Listen to Jeremiah (17:14): "If I am to be healed, it is thou, Lord, must heal me." Such also was the prayer of the woman when she touched his garment: "If I am to find deliverance, it is thou must deliver me; thou art all my boast."

102. The faithful are often tempted, and so somebody may taunt you, saying (Jer 17:15): "What has become of the Lord's word? We are waiting to see it accomplished!" People said to the Lord himself (Mt 27:42): "He has but to come down from the cross; here and now, and we will believe in him. He trusted in God; let God, if he favors him, succor him now." If somebody insults you like that, to draw you into idle talk, do not reply to him. Christ did not reply to such things. Address only Christ. If you speak to them, they will not believe you: if you question them, they will not reply. Speak only to the Lord (Jer 17:15): "Where is the word of the Lord. Let it come." (RSVCE)

103. When the woman spoke so, her issue of blood ceased. There is no weariness in following where Christ leads, for he calls to himself those who labor that they may have rest. So, we must follow him. In this we shall not labor in vain (Num 23:23): "It is no false God that Jacob worships." And Isaiah says (40:31): "Those who trusted in the Lord will . . . never grow weary of hastening."

104. When Christ asked who had touched him, we can imagine the woman saying: "Why do you ask, Lord? You already know. The words that come from my lips are already before your eyes, and so I have no shame in confessing my sins". Jeremiah says: "They must be abashed, and I vindicated." (Jer 17:18).

105. Peter too was not ashamed to say (Lk 5:8): "Leave me to myself, Lord; I am a sinner." This wise and prudent man, on whom the Church and her office of teaching were to be built, thought it best not to be lifted up by the successful outcome of his action. So he said: "Leave me to myself, Lord." He does not ask to be deserted, but to be humbled.

106. Paul too was unashamed of the sting in his flesh which was given to him that he might not become proud (2 Cor 12:7). Pride must be seductive if Paul too fears it; it must be perilous if he seeks to avoid it. He was not the sort to fall easily, this man who feared that revelations might make him proud. Like a good athlete he was glad, that by chastising the body he could achieve health of the soul.

Prudent thoughts

107. You too, if you know that the divine gifts are abundant in you, fear for your virtue; give thanks to God and learn to think of your body as the ballast of a ship, preventing the wind of pride from seizing you amid the waves of this world. The bee, when it suspects any movement of the wind, wisely takes little pebbles with it when rising into the clouds, so that the wind may not sweep its little wings off course. Paul and Barnabas felt themselves weighed down like that even in face of adoration. Be careful, virgin, like the little bee, and do not let the breezes of the world puff you up in your flight.

108. For the soul does have its flight. It is said (Is 60:8): "Who are those that come, swift as the clouds, as doves flying home to the dovecot?" The spiritual flight of the soul traverses the whole world in a short time. Prudent thoughts are detached, and the more they ascend towards the high and divine, the more their flight is unhindered by earthly weight. Adhering to God and ever keeping an inner image of him, the soul, steadying its turbulent passions, ascends into that ethereal and pure place on the beat of spiritual wings. It then despises everything in this world, and intent only on heavenly virtues, is borne above the world. Above the world is justice, above the world is chastity, above the world is goodness and wisdom. These virtues, even if you find them in this world, are nevertheless above it.

109. Above the world was Christ, justice itself, when the devil offered him all the kingdoms of the world and all its glory. Above the world was Christ who touched nothing of the world. He said (Jn 14:30): "One is coming who has power over the world, but no hold over me." Learn then to be above the world while still in it. Though you must bear your body let your inner soul fly. He who bears God in his body is above the world.

Rising above earthly things

110. If we cannot fully imitate him who was God let us imitate the Apostles, whom the world held in hatred because they were not of the world. Imitate these and follow them. Perhaps you think it a very difficult thing to get above the world by your own powers. You are right. The Apostles managed to rise above the world, by following the Lord not as his equals but as his pupils. Be a pupil of Christ; strive to imitate him, and his prayer for you will be the same as for them (Jn

17:20): "It is not only for them that I pray; I pray for those who are to find faith in me through their word; that they may all be one." The Lord wants us to form a unity with him above the world, in one chastity, one will, one goodness, one grace. These are the things that nourish and strengthen the upper flight of the soul.

111. Let us lose no time then in rising from the things of earth. It is by using wings that you give them strength. Flight too is helped on by the delight of the soul. If the soul desires to follow God and to live in the house of the Lord, feeding on his delight and nourished by the wonders of the heavenly virtues, it will leave behind envy, which is foreign to the choir of angels, and bodily desires which have no place in the temple of God. If we are the temple of God, we must do away with all material cares in our hearts.

112. Perhaps I seem to be talking the language of philosophers or poets: chariots and horses and wings of the soul. But they took over these images from us. A verse in Ezekiel shows us that we draw on our own store of thought in these things (Ez 1:4): "I looked round me to find that a stormy wind had sprung up from the north, driving a great cloud before it; and this cloud had fire caught up in it, that fringed it with radiance; and there in the heart of it, in the very heart of the fire was a glow like amber, that enclosed four living figures."

113. These are the four animals. We must notice the description of them (Ez 1:10): "As for the appearance of their faces, each had the face of a man, yet each of the four looked like a lion when seen from the right, like an ox when seen from the left, like an eagle when seen from above. So much for their faces; each had two wings spread out above him."

114. This serves also for a description of the soul, whose four animals are four affections. This is not what we spoke of previously. In that former case the souls were in process of training, but here the soul is already perfect. Those other souls were on their way to heaven, but this one is already there with the Word of God. It has its four affections, in the likeness of man and lion and ox and eagle. We normally take these figures to represent the four Gospels. But here they stand for the four affections: the rational in the figure of the man, the irascible in the figure of the lion, the concupiscent in the ox, and the discerning in the eagle.

115. The Greek philosophers held that every wise man has four faculties: reason, anger, desire, discernment. The Latins have four corresponding terms: prudence, fortitude, temperance, and justice. Prudence belongs to reason. Fortitude, cognate with anger, instils bravery and contempt of death. Temperance through the bond of holy love and the contemplation of heavenly mysteries overcomes bodily desire. Justice, seated on her throne, perceives and explores all things; living for others rather than for herself, she seeks not her own advantage but the common good. That is why the soul practicing justice is pictured as an eagle: she flies above everything earthly, intent only on the heavenly mysteries, and she gains the glory of resurrection as her reward. And so it was said to her (Ps 103:5): "He restores thy youth as the eagle's plumage is restored."

116. David too shows us the soul soaring upon her spiritual wings, comparing her to a bird (Ps 123:7): "Safe, like a bird rescued from the fowler's snare; the snare is broken and we are safe." In another place (Ps 11:1): "My trust is in the Lord; how is it that you say to me: Escape, like a frightened sparrow, to the hillside?" You see, the soul has its wings and can

free itself from the earth. These are not an arrangement of material feathers but the ordered span of good deeds. The Psalm says to the Lord (Ps 57:1): "I will take refuge under the shelter of thy wings." The Lord's hands nailed to the Cross were like wings extended in flight, and his heavenly deeds were like a refreshing shade, that of eternal salvation tempering the burning heat of this world.

117. Since the power of flight has been given to us, we must rouse up in ourselves the grace of God and, forgetting the things that are behind, hasten forward to the goal in front of us. We must shun ambitions, honors, and the disturbances of the world; otherwise, as in the story of Icarus, the heat of the sun may melt the wax on our wings and bring us down. Admittedly this is only a fable; but it does tell us with a certain poetic charm that the man of mature wisdom suffers nothing in his flight through the world; but the levity of youth, affected by worldly desires, may incur a melting of the wax, a dissolution of good works through forgetfulness of the truth, and so may crash to earth.

118. Flight does not come easy to all. In the passage of life, the soul's main difficulty is the discord of the animals inside it. But if our actions maintain due order among themselves, the Prophet will again see in us his vision of one wheel on the earth with four animals yoked to it (Ez 1:15). Yes, Ezekiel will see it again for he is still alive and able to see. He will see (Ez 1:15) "wheel within wheel" turning on the earth without hindrance. The wheel upon the earth is the life of the body yoked to the virtue of the soul and turning in an even course in accord with the evangelical precepts. The wheel within wheel is as it were a life within life, a life of sanctity, for the life of the Saints is ever harmonious within itself, past and present. Or the wheel may signify the eternal life within the life of the body.

Spiritual fishing with the hook of doctrine

119. When that harmony is there, the divine voice will be heard and there will appear seated on a throne the image of a man. This man is the Word, for (Jn 1:14) "the Word made flesh." This man is the driver of the inner animals, the charioteer of our habits. According to our merits, the Word will ascend chariot or mountain or ship. The ship he boards is that of the Apostles, that of the fisherman Peter. That good ship sails out on to the deep, severing itself from unbelievers. That ship was picked by Christ for his teaching of the crowd to show that the Church is a ship, which with Christ's cross spread for its sail moves safely through the sea of this world on the wind of the Spirit.

120. In this boat Peter fishes. His orders are to use nets at one time and hook at another. This is that mystery of spiritual fishing where he is ordered to cast the hook of doctrine into the world. He takes as his first catch the martyr Stephen, who holds the coin of Christ within himself, for Christ's martyr is the treasure of the Church. That first martyr taken from the sea into heaven was caught by Peter in the service of the altar, caught with the hook and not the net, taken from the stream of his own blood up into heaven. His coin was in his mouth, for he confessed Christ, and what other treasure can be within us except the Word of God? The perfect fisherman uses both net and hook: the net gathers the multitude, the hook takes the individual. I would be happy to bite that hook and have it pierce my lips, getting salvation from its sweet wound.

121. Enter, my daughters, the nets of the Apostles; they are let down not by the orders of men but by the voice of God. In the net of spiritual wisdom and doctrine is the kingdom of heaven, for we read (Mt 13:47): "The kingdom of heaven is like a net that was cast into the sea."

The meaning of deep water

122. In the Gospel of today, the feast of Saints Peter and Paul, you heard the Lord Jesus saying to Simon (Lk 5:4): "Stand out into the deep water and let down your nets for a catch." Up to then Peter had fished on the lake, but he could hardly "stand out into the deep" for the lake was shallow. The Scripture says nothing about it being deep. The meaning then of the word "deep" must be that of the proverb (Prov 20:5): "Prudent counsel is a well buried deep in man's heart." In that deep are no shallows. Put out, then, the ship of your preaching and of your faith into the deep of man's heart. Using this language, Christ calls Peter to the Church. In Matthew's Gospel, the call had simply been "Come and follow me; I will make you into fishers of men." (Mt 4:19).

123. Another meaning hides in the words "Stand out into the deep." Peter, you know, had really been on the sand when in the Synagogue, for the waters of the land of Judah were far from deep. The Samaritan woman made a reference to deep water when she said, "The well is deep; how then can you provide living water?" (John 4:11). Peter could not launch into the deep while he was still in the faith of the Jews, who could not even draw the waters of a well. And so, Christ's words to him were: "Stand out into the deep water." That means advance towards Christ; for Christ is the height and depth of which Zachary spoke to his son John (Lk 1:76): "And thou, my child, will be known for a prophet of the most high." Launch out then towards Christ. He is well described in the words of Paul (Rom 11:33): "How deep is the mind of God's wisdom, of his knowledge!" Stand out into that deep. He is deep, and high above the deep, protecting and raising aloft.

124. The deep waters then are where Christ is, where there is faith and the fear of the Lord (Ps 77:16): "The waters saw

thee, O God, the waters trembled at sight of thee." With the Jews there was no deep water, because there was no depth of heart, and so the Lord said, "This people honors me with its lips, but its heart is far from me." (Mt 15:8). Christ desires to be in the heart: "Jonas was three days and three nights in the belly of the sea-beast, and the Son of Man will be three days and three nights in the heart of the earth." (Mt 12:40).

125. He is talking of faith when he says: "Stand out into the deep water," for Peter replies (Lk 5:5): "Master, we have toiled all the night and caught nothing; but at thy word I will let down the net." It was darkness for Peter until he saw Christ. Up to then day had not reached him for he had not yet seen that true light. The Synagogue is night, the Church is day. Paul says (Rom 13:12): "The night is far on its course; day draws near." That is the good light which disperses the darkness of infidelity and brings the daylight of faith. Peter and Paul are that day. The Holy Spirit proclaims now, on their birthday (Ps 19:2–4): "Each day echoes its secret to the next," which means that from the inner treasure of their hearts they preach the faith of Christ. Each of them is a good day, bearing the true light to us.

126. We read all this in the Gospel, and perhaps in heaven today Christ and Peter are saying the same words. Continually Peter does his fishing and continually the Lord says to him: "Stand out on to the deep water." I seem too, to hear Peter replying: "Master we have toiled all night and have caught nothing." Only a few people came here last night to celebrate the vigil. If our devotion is weak, Peter must keep toiling. And Paul too, for you have heard him today saying (2 Cor 11:2): "Does anyone feel a scruple? I share it." Do not make the Apostles labor for you in this way. That is

the point of their words: 'We have toiled all the night and caught nothing.' None of our rich people has been keeping the fast. For these today, Peter has fitting words: "Look anxiously, then, to the ordering of your lives while your stay on earth lasts. What was the ransom that freed you from the vain observances of ancestral tradition? You know that the ransom was not paid in earthly currency, silver or gold; it was paid in the precious blood of Christ; no lamb was ever so pure and spotless a victim." (1 Pet 1:17–18) .Gold or silver, then, is not your ransom, but tested faith, much more precious than the metals that perish.

127. The good servant tries to return what his master paid for him. But you, daughter, do not get ready gold or silver; it was not with such coin that Christ bought you. But have the true price ready. You may not be pressed for it, but you still owe it; Christ paid his blood for you, and you owe him yours. He paid for you; now you should pay for yourself. Through sin we were all given as security to a bad creditor; we signed the contract of guilt and incurred the debt of blood. But the Lord Jesus came and shed his own blood for us, a debt too great to be adequately repaid.

128. Yet the good slave tries to make up his debt to his lord, and if he is unable to do that at least it is his duty not to appear unworthy of the price paid for him. Carry yourself in a manner worthy of the price Christ paid for you, so that he who cleansed and redeemed you may not come and find you in sin and say to you (Ps 30:9): "How will it profit thee to take my life? I can but go down into the grave."

129. Do not wonder at this phrase "go down into the grave." His flesh, as we read elsewhere, sees no corruption. Though he went down into the place of corruption, penetrating the regions of death, in his case there could be no corruption.

130. To return to our text. I want you to pray that I also may hear the words: "Stand out on the deep water and let down your nets for a catch." Who, without the aid of God, could fish for this people in the middle of the world's tempests and squalls? But when the Lord at his pleasure orders us to let down our nets, a great catch is made, filling even a second ship; for more than one church is filled with the throng of the chaste. It is fortunate that the Lord, foreseeing my difficulties, has sent companions to aid me. I have by me the fisherman from the church of Bologna, Bishop Eusebius, who is an expert in the task. Lord, I now ask you to give me fish, seeing that you have given me helpers.

The nets of the Apostles

131. The nets we use are not our own, they are those of the Apostles. Daughters, may you all be gathered like a shoal into these nets, into the folds of the apostolic teaching. May Peter give you life! He who intervened on behalf of the widows will do it even more for the virgin (Acts 9:39). We read in *Acts* that he could not bear the weeping of the widows, but moved by their tears, raised their benefactress, Dorcas, from the dead. May Paul also give you life who demanded honor to be given you and said "They will do well to remain in the same state as myself" (1 Cor 7:8). He entices you with honors, teaches you with knowledge, invites you with his example. May Peter and John give you life, those two who left all things to follow Christ.

132. Note the success Peter the fisherman had. While making his own living on the sea he found the true life of all men. He left his boat and found God, left his oars, and found the Word. He let down his net and caught faith; he raised his net and raised all mankind. He gave up the sea and found heaven.

Though himself tossed on a disturbed sea, he made firm as a rock the minds of men swaying in a sea of uncertainty.

133. Let us think more about that fisherman's art that our faith in its power may be fuller. Though his occupation was lowly, he was to become a great preacher of the Gospel. Though poor, he would be all the richer in virtue. Though of little account as far as earthly honors go, he would be of supreme importance through his faith. The less we can heed him as a mere fisherman, the more we can take what he says as being not his own, but God's. His lowly condition even helps him: it removes all expectation of earthly knowledge and increases our belief that his wisdom is of the Spirit. A man who has not studied the law and yet understands it, has it living within himself. He who has no knowledge of the law and yet can speak of things above it must derive his knowledge from the Maker of the law.

134. What a sudden dignity exalts two fishermen! On Tabor, the mountain of the Lord, the one is compared to Moses, the giver of the law, the other to Elias, its executor. Remember that Moses went above all earthly things, all the heights of worldly wisdom, and penetrated right up to heaven by the acumen of his soul. But the soul of John, the fisherman, unblinded by cloud, never hemmed in by things temporal, did not stop at the mysteries of heaven, but soaring above all bodily substance, saw the Word with God, and saw that the Word was God. And Peter did not waver when he saw with the eyes of the flesh the Son of God in the form of man, knowing that by the Incarnation, a human body was taken into divinity and had its nature joined with that of its Maker.

135. In the phrases (Gen 1:3) "God said" and "God made," Moses referred to the Father and the Son. He had knowledge

of the mystery, but I have been ignorant of it. After the giving of the Law the chosen people erred, though with the Gospel they found faith again. The grace of God appears in different manifestations: in Moses, who was able to describe the creation of the world; and in John, who despised the world.